The Authentic Entrepreneur

True Stories from the Heart of Business

Stephen Kirk

GeniusMedia
CREATING KNOWLEDGE

2021

The Authentic Entrepreneur

True Stories from the Heart of Business

First Edition: February 2021

ISBN 978-1-908293-55-8

Genius Media 2021

Genius Media

B1502

PO Box 15113

Birmingham

B2 2NJ

www.geniusmedia.pub

books@geniusmedia.pub

www.stephenkirk.org

Contents

Acknowledgements

This book seems to have a life of its own and has propelled me along at breakneck speed, but it would never have happened without the suggestion of Paul Boross.

I'd like to thank him and to my wonderful interviewees: Toby Clarke, Gaelle Kennedy, Aron Hughes, Asher Budwig, Jason Kirk, Monica Dodi, Bernard Frei, Sam Sutton, Marcus Watson, Tracy Gray, and Sir Harry Solomon.

Also, thanks to Tania Slowe who introduced me to The Prince's Trust and Karis Eaglestone from The Prince's Trust for her support.

Help with proof-reading came from Larry Smith, Becca Pronchick, Jane Cheshire-Allen, Jim Platt, and Lesley Moss.

My wife, Luiza Kirk supported and comforted me when I realised the enormity of the challenge I had taken on and she was a magnificent sounding board.

Last but not least, thanks to Peter Freeth at Genius Media for generously supporting this project in favour of The Prince's Trust.

Introduction

This is a book for Authentic Entrepreneurs. Those who are not only interested in making money, but also in giving something back and growing in the process.

Apart from recounting my own story, I have selected entrepreneurs at various stages of their enterprises and differing aspirations and visions.

This is not a business manual – there are plenty of those in the marketplace. But I hope it will fuel your ideas. The interviews broadly cover starting out, staying in a family business, serial entrepreneurialism, raising funds, mentoring, philanthropy, and Angel investment. However, almost every interview contains elements of these.

But first I'm going to take you through my own journey.

Every life is unique in a world that seems to require conformity. To be an entrepreneur you have to forge your own path. This is the first and perhaps most difficult challenge.

My own case was no different.

I'm very lucky because several years ago I achieved my business goals. I did slightly better than I ever would have dreamed possible.

I wanted to make enough money to feed myself and my family, to have a debt-free house, and to be able to retire should I wish, with enough savings to travel comfortably to exotic destinations. I now share my expertise through coaching and mentoring.

I started with zero business experience, no money behind me, no idea what a balance sheet was, and without reading a single business guru book. My philosophy continues to be 'follow your heart but consult your brain'.

Strangely, simultaneously with achieving my goals in 2000, I was diagnosed with a life-threatening illness from which I completely recovered but it sent me in a completely new direction.

I'm told I'm wise having worked at the coalface of business and consequently I was asked to sit on the Boards of ten companies as a Non-Executive Director but after 16 years, I decided to take a break whilst Luiza, my wife, and I travel the world in search of Paradise!

I'm told I'm funny. I've done two stand-up comedy courses but since I don't like late nights, stand-up was never going to play a big part in my future. But of course, everything's going online so who knows?

However, occasionally I feel that I 'should' be doing something more.

Then I chatted with my good friend Paul Boross, who is a keynote speaker, comic, musician, executive coach – you name it! I challenged him to help me decide how I would like to spend the next few years.

He asked me a few searching questions and the best I could answer was that I wanted to be interviewed on the Chris Evans Breakfast Show and be an occasional speaker on retreats.

Paul, being Paul, suggested I should write this book to develop a 'platform'.

So, I began to write. It was bloody hard work and I was not enjoying it. Moreover, every time somebody asked why I was writing it I replied, 'Because Paul told me to!'

I appreciated this was pretty pathetic, but a platform didn't appeal to me and there was no real hope of a self-published book covering its publishing costs.

Then I had my first brainwave. I was going to approach well-known entrepreneurs. You know, the likes of Richard Branson, Jeff Bezos, Steve Jobs (via a psychic – only partially joking).

But I realised that apart from the difficulty of getting hold of these folks (particularly Steve Jobs), I really needed people whom I could easily meet.

What if I simply interviewed authentic entrepreneurs I know of and ask them to share their experiences?

People you can easily relate to and maybe guide you on your way. Newbies, serial entrepreneurs, and everything in between. Those who are powering on from venture to venture and those who have now devoted themselves to mentoring and helping others.

Then came Brainwave Number Two.

I interviewed my cousin Jason Kirk, who is the only person of my generation who has remained associated with the family optical business.

At the end of the interview, Jason told me that he had just self-published a book of kids' poems with all the money donated to a nurses' charity.

And that revelation excited me!

I would donate my royalties to The Prince's Trust, (registered charity England and Wales 1079675 and Scotland SC041198) whose patron is His Royal Highness, The Prince of Wales. They run a range of training programs, providing practical and financial support to build young people's confidence and skills. A donation has been made to the Prince's Trust from the cover price of this book.

Finally, I was approached by Peter Freeth at Genius Media, who kindly offered to publish this book and also donate his royalties.

I do hope you enjoy reading my book and please contact me if you'd like to chat further: stephenmkirk1@gmail.com

Part 1: Welcome to my World

I wanted to start a business where I could be of service to those around me - to my staff, to suppliers, and to provide something which was of use or at least made people laugh! And of course, to make a living.

During my journey, I made several discoveries about myself and I also learnt a great deal more about how the business world functions.

I should emphasise that I had absolutely no business experience when I started. I had come out of university with a Computer Science degree. It was one of the first. I was fascinated by the idea of Artificial Intelligence. But in 1975 when I graduated, computers were at the very beginning and the world was not ready for them!

The computer I used was called Atlas and it took up a huge floor of the new Manchester University Computer Science Building. Yet it probably had the processing power of today's laptop!

My journey shows a degree of magic and it is the first time that I have felt able to share with anyone my adventures in this way.

Normally I would either relate the business part to my business associates or the magic part to those who are interested in personal development and growth.

But today I'm going to give you the whole story because it might provide you with some lessons and inspiration for your future.

I'm also going to distil what I've learnt, hopefully in a thought-provoking way. Also, there are stories from inspirational entrepreneurs from around the world.

Let's start…

In 1977, I was on a meditation course, which was to last four months, when I began to get the urge to go into business. This was a complete surprise to me. I was set to become one of the first Teachers of Transcendental Meditation (TM, which I still practice to this day).

I had enrolled on the course because I wanted to change the world. I was young and full of hope that the world could be a better place for all – but only if more people turned inwards, meditated, and resolved their inner conflicts.

So, this insistent inner voice whispering that I should go into business was a total surprise.

TM is one of the most important components of my life alongside my relationship with my wife, my family and friends.

I had almost failed my first-year Uni exams because I was so stressed, so I realised that I had to do something about my neurosis.

My mother had mental illness and I didn't want to go the same way. So, I hunted around for something that would keep me calm and discovered TM because of a strange but fortuitous coincidence…

When I was growing up my parents insisted that I attend Hebrew classes at South Tottenham Synagogue, led by Rabbi Joseph Unterman.

Then at Uni, the Jewish Centre Rabbi was Alan Unterman, and Alan remembered that his father, Rabbi Joseph had mentioned me to him. Apparently, he had said, 'If you ever meet Stephen Kirk, look after him because he's a special person'. High praise indeed and I can assure you totally inexplicable!

Rabbi Alan informed me that there was a Jewish teacher of TM coming to Manchester and advised me to learn to restore me to calmness.

There was no way on earth that my parents would have allowed me to learn TM under normal circumstances because for them it was a Hindu practice. But because Rabbi Alan had given it his seal of approval, they reluctantly agreed.

My parents had very fixed ideas about how I should live my life, what I should do for a living, and whom I should marry.

There was a family optical business called Kirk Brothers set up by Grandpa Percy and Uncle Sid, and I had been expected to join that.

But I had a little stroke of luck in that I developed an eye phobia.

I realised this when Dad arranged a tour around City University. It was THE place to learn optics and that was where I was expected to study. Grandpa Percy had invented several optical gadgets, which were on display there.

The professor taking us round showed us my grandfather's inventions and then told us that contact lenses were the new craze.

On the way home, I had to admit to Dad that I had an eye phobia. This was secretly quite amusing to me as I marvelled at how clever my subconscious was. There was no way it would allow me to become an optician!

But my father was extremely disappointed, and it led to him selling the remnant of the business that he had inherited from Grandpa.

Then I had to think about what I wanted to do.

I was interested in psychology and technology and thought if I could tie them together, that would give me a satisfying existence. I was also far-sighted enough to realise that a degree in Computer Science was THE future, albeit, in those days, no one had any idea of how much computers would change our lives.

Therefore, I applied for the Computer Science course at Manchester University and was accepted.

Luckily TM made such a difference to me that I sailed through the final two years of my degree. And then there was an ironic moment when I did so well at my finals that my tutor asked for my exams to be re-marked. She thought I could not have possibly achieved such a high grade!

Never in my life have I heard of a tutor asking for a student's exams to be marked down because they had done better than expected. Luckily, however, the results were correct. And although I didn't do well enough to get a First, for me it was a remarkable achievement.

Before starting Uni, I had wanted to avoid my parents having to pay tuition fees. Not that this was an issue for them particularly, but I wanted to be independent.

I had sent out letters to organisations I thought might be interested in sponsoring me through University, given that I was to study Computer Science. And lo and behold, I received a reply from the Electricity Council, which was then the UK Government body regulating the Electricity Supply Industry.

My letter arrived on the day that the Head of Personnel was looking for a young person to sponsor through university and bring them into the organisation to help with the upcoming arrival of computers.

Thus, I landed a job as a computer programmer, for what was then a very good salary. The deal was that I worked for the Electricity Council during the Uni holidays and pledged to stay for at least three years after I graduated.

Unfortunately, those years at the Electricity Council were perhaps the least fulfilling of my working career. My job was to write computer programs predicting electricity faults such as those caused by birds flying into power cables!

Each program would be typed out on cards and delivered to the Computer Room at the University of London by courier and returned a few hours later. Any errors in the program would then be corrected and the whole process repeated.

This would go on until eventually the computer program worked correctly and I would move on to the next program.

Luckily, the Tate Gallery was next to my office so I spent many happy hours there, which fostered my life-long interest in art. There I would attend lectures from Simon Wilson including one on the infamous Bricks by Carl Andre.

I would while away hours on the steps of the Gallery hoping to chat up an attractive female tourist. A fantasy that was never to be fulfilled.

Meanwhile, in the Electricity Council, there was a Staff Canteen and Coffee Lounge, a library, and various recreational activities. You might say, this was like the Apple campus today!

My desk in the newly opened Millbank Tower was probably the only one without a Thames View and instead, I had to stare out at the Air Conditioning Unit.

My social life was pretty unexciting too. There were a couple of Jewish Youth Clubs that my parents allowed me to attend and there I got to know Lesley who was also in a different class at my school. She was to become my first wife.

There was a small thrill in that an article I had written was accepted by a Jewish Youth Magazine, Mosaic. The magazine editor, David Dangoor, would have regular editorial meetings in his apartment behind the Royal Albert Hall and there I would have my first encounter with 'sophisticated' Jews.

I felt completely out of my depth. This lot seemed to read books, go to museums and concerts. Luckily, I could talk about Art but apart from that I simply made people laugh. When in doubt make'em laugh!

In that vein, I started to apply for tickets to BBC comedy shows. Queueing for one show I met a chap, who had some sort of inside track and a regular ticket supply to I'm Sorry I'll Read That Again, which was a spinoff from the Cambridge Footlights, with a cast including John Cleese.

These shows kindled my desire to move into media if I possibly could, but how?

It also made me realise that the Electricity Council was no path for fulfilment and that TM had been such a turning point for me that perhaps it would offer a career path especially as I couldn't think of anything else!

Mind you whilst at the Council, I did see an advert for a programmer at the soon to be opened London Weekend Television(LWT), but I didn't apply because it was based in Stonebridge Park, a London suburb at the back of beyond. Little did I know LWT was soon to move to a prestigious site on London's South Bank, and that the Producer of I'm Sorry, Humphrey Barclay was to join it. My life might have taken a completely different course had I applied.

Anyway, back then The Beatles were promoting TM and its Founder Maharishi Mahesh Yogi, young, laughing and charismatic was encouraging large meditation groups to foster World Peace.

Lesley had learnt TM with me and had qualified as a schoolteacher.

We decided we wanted to carve out new lives for ourselves and join a TM Teacher Training Course.

This was not cheap so in a move that understandably infuriated my parents, and probably rather shocked hers, we sold the apartment my parents had bought us as a generous wedding present, attempted to return them the money – I can't honestly remember if we succeeded – and used the profit to pay the £4000 for the course.

But we also needed somewhere to rent until the course began.

I had always wanted to live in Bohemian Hampstead rather than suburban North London. It was August Bank Holiday and incredibly quiet. We decided to buy The Hampstead and Highgate Express and look through it for property rentals.

One apartment jumped out at us. It overlooked Hampstead Heath and was quoted at £30 a week – which was incredibly cheap for the area.

We rang the owner from a public call box. The woman who answered was delighted to hear from us. She hadn't realised that it was a Bank Holiday and we were the only people who had contacted her!

She and her husband lectured at Beirut University. They wanted a reliable couple to look after their flat in their absence. But more fundamentally they were Quakers and were extremely enthusiastic when we told them about our TM plans. A deal was done. It just so happened that our course roughly coincided with their trips back to London, so it was a perfect match.

I hadn't intended to resign from the Electricity Council but had negotiated a three-month leave of absence to attend the course. They thought I was mad, but they were up for it.

It was 1977 and meditation, mindfulness and yoga were not in the public vernacular, and were regarded with a high degree of scepticism and even hostility.

We began the course. It was billed as being three months. It ended up being peripatetic and starting in Kent because Maharishi decided to extend it to four months and no venue was available for the entire time.

The Electricity Council flatly refused to grant me the extra month and threatened to send the Personnel Manager down to the course to knock some sense into me! But I insisted by letter that this was pointless, and they accepted my resignation.

By this point, my friends, parents, and in-laws all thought I had completely lost touch with reality!

The course itself was intensive. We had thirty minutes a week spare to do our laundry! It consisted of four hours of daily meditation plus countless lectures, many consisting of Maharishi's videos and then tests.

Two weeks into the course my mother attempted suicide. I had emphasised to my parents that we were not allowed to leave and were we to do so we would not qualify, nor would we receive a refund. But obviously, we had no choice but to return to London to Mum who was in intensive care.

We were given two weeks to return. As it happened, she recovered amazingly quickly (or so it seemed) and we went back to the course with her well-being very much on our minds and calling her regularly.

It seemed like a miracle had taken place. She was her old self. When she was 'up' she was lively and had a keen sense of humour and had even applied for a part-time job at Marks and Spencer Department Store.

We relaxed a tad and focused on our lessons.

Then after two months, we had to change the retreat location. The men were to be sent to Devon and the women to Loch Rannoch in the Scottish Highlands. We were the only married couple and I had to plead not to be split up from Lesley, especially given my mother's precarious health.

I was therefore allowed to join Lesley and twenty other young women!

As the weeks went by, I began to fantasise about starting a business. I kept pushing the thought away but it was getting stronger.

We 'graduated', but shortly after there was a knock on our bedroom door. My mother was dead, and we had to return to London for the funeral. I was spaced out from the months of meditation so the whole event seemed like a dream. The post-mortem, funeral, seven days of mourning, and then the return to 'normal' life.

Thankfully thanks to the Quaker couple (plus my sister) we had somewhere to stay and we eventually settled into our new Hampstead life.

We had gone on the course to open a TM centre, but I had returned motherless and with a thirst for business for which I was uniquely unqualified!

Frankly, I had no idea what to do next career-wise. I was just a humble computer programmer and I still couldn't understand where this feeling was coming from, but it was getting stronger and stronger.

I was all fired up to become an entrepreneur.

Somehow, I got an introduction to a recruitment consultant, Doug Sneddon.

Doug asked me what sort of job I was looking for, so I made something up! I said that I had been a Computer

Programmer and Systems Analyst. But what I really wanted was to get a job involving technology and television.

He looked at me in astonishment and announced that he had just the job for me! He had just written it up and put it in his file. Remember, everything was on paper in those days.

Then and there he made a phone call and ordered me to go around the corner to Lincoln's Inn Fields to meet a gentleman called George Bulmer who would tell me all about it.

I marched to 17 Lincoln's Inn Fields where George was waiting for me. He was dressed like an off-duty army major in a pinstripe suit. A very tall, thin man sporting a moustache. And his first words were 'Are you a Mason?' Well, I wasn't but he said he would sort that out, although he never did!

And I repeated to him what I had told Doug.

To my amazement, he said, 'How would you like a salary of £30,000 a year and an office in Amsterdam where we would provide you with a company flat and of course, a company car. What car do you currently drive?'

I told him a Ford Cortina.

I didn't tell him I'd been looking after a beaten-up Ford Cortina for a friend who had nowhere to park near his house. 'No, that will never do! You must have a Chrysler Alpine', which at the time was a fashionable model.

So, by the end of that day, I'd been promised a job and flat in Amsterdam, a very large salary for the time, and a company car.

All this was a magical sequence of events because it showed me that after almost four months of meditation, I was on the right track to realise my full potential.

For a few years, the magic would continue with great intensity and mystery.

For instance, just before leaving for Amsterdam, I was rung up by George and told that the guy I was supposed to report to in Amsterdam had resigned and now I would be managing the whole of Europe from the Amsterdam office!

The company was Aregon International, which was itself backed by a Government Quango called the National Enterprise Board.

My job was to sell the predecessor to the internet called Prestel, which had been developed by the British Post Office, throughout Europe. My clients would include the Italian State News Agency and similar information providers.

The technology itself had the generic name of videotext. Once it was the hot thing like the internet but now almost totally forgotten!

It enabled a television set to be two-way, but of course in a rudimentary manner. A Prestel box was connected to a television set and then to a phone line to create interactivity. I was told I could work out of British Embassies when not in Amsterdam. I was particularly fond of the Embassy in Rome, which is a spectacular building in magnificent grounds, and I got on very well with the Commercial Attaché, Derek Rhodes, who would arrange an office for me whenever I was there.

Each Commercial Attaché I visited also hosted events on my behalf, sometimes attended by the Ambassador. As a consequence, I performed incredibly well in my new position as a Super Salesman.

However, Lesley became pregnant with our first child in Amsterdam and she understandably wanted to return to London to give birth. Consequently, I had to resign because the one place Aregon was not allowed to trade was the

United Kingdom where the British Post Office had the monopoly.

It was years later that I realised that perhaps this remarkable series of events whereby I could work out of embassies might have been because the company was a front for MI6!

It's worth going on a little detour into the future to demonstrate the Ark of Coincidence. Perhaps there's more going on than we imagine? Perhaps we all have a 'right path' and a destiny?

At Aregon, despite my young age, but demonstrable sales success, I was assigned a young Oxford graduate by the name of Bernard Lunn. Bernard was urbane and thoughtful. I was neither and we got on extremely well.

After I left Aregon I spent thirty years in other activities until I found myself on the Board of The Ink Factory, founded by John Le Carre's sons, Simon and Stephen Cornwell.

I had recently re-connected with Bernard through social media and Bernard had replied to my message with 'Is that the legendary Stephen Kirk?' The word 'legendary' struck me.

When Bernard's email arrived, Luiza (now my wife) and I were spending a winter in Ojai, California where Stephen Cornwell lives and Stephen hosted a tea party. We were chatting to him, when someone at the far end of the room, nowhere near us, shouted out 'legendary' for no reason we could fathom.

This re-kindled my suspicions that Aregon might have been a front for MI6. I related my story to Stephen Cornwell and when I got to the name Bernard Lunn, he stopped me.

'Is he the son of Peter Lunn?' Stephen asked.

'No idea… why?'

'Because Peter Lunn was a super spy and the model for Smiley in Tinker Tailor'.

That was John Le Carre's most famous spy novel!

Stephen explained that often MI6 would set up front operations to give them legitimacy and the technology I was peddling – two-way communications – was ideal for spying – wasn't it?

As I said, we will never know…and Bernard is indeed Peter Lunn's son!

Anyway, once I'd resigned from Aregon we returned to London where I worked for John Clemens whom I'd met during my Aregon business dealings. He had established AGB Cable and Viewdata which was to develop connections in the fledgling British cable TV industry as well as polling for TV companies.

One day, John informed me of a new research development tool called Acorn whereby each neighbourhood in the United Kingdom was graded according to various parameters, which related to the people that lived there. It was a very simple but powerful concept. Your neighbour almost certainly has similar buying habits to you.

I realised that we could plot the potential take-up in specific franchise areas for cable TV because each area had different attributes in terms of income, expenditure and passions.

This was a genius idea as far as my company was concerned and we rapidly developed a research product and gained business from all the prospective cable TV operators. One of these, Windsor Television, offered me a Non-Executive Directorship. This gave me real cable TV experience at the cutting edge.

But despite earning a very good salary I had two young kids to support and times were quite tough financially. Fate intervened and I was to resign over an argument with John over his fridge. Or rather fridges.

You see he had a flat in Italy and he had graciously offered my family the chance to stay there provided we adhere to one rule. And that was to leave the fridge door open when we left. Well, when we got to the flat there were TWO fridges. One had the door open and the other closed.

In those days you did not make long-distance calls. Not that we could because there was no landline there and of course mobile phones and the Internet had not been invented.

When we vacated, we left the fridges as we had found them. I told John on our return and he went ballistic because I had not followed his instructions. Apparently, I should have left both doors open.

Well, he shouted at me so angrily that I decided to resign with immediate effect! Lesley seemed to take it all calmly but now I needed to work out my future career.

In the short term, I worked for John on a freelance basis to complete an on-air voting contract he had with Granada Television, but I needed a plan B.

Soon it seemed obvious (to me at least!) that I should found a cable TV franchise in the London borough of Camden, where we lived. I had no fear in those days. I took out an advert in the Hampstead and Highgate Express, asking if anybody was interested in helping me and soon, I had a variety of folk, mainly retired, who were keen on becoming Board members of my newly incorporated company, Cable Camden.

We needed to raise money, so I approached the computer company Logica, whose Founder Philip Hughes lived locally, McNicholas Construction, Mercury Communications and the Private Equity firm 3i amongst several other companies and before I knew it, we'd raised enough to bid for the franchise!

I was the only one with cable TV experience because I was already on the Board of Windsor Television. Moreover, the franchise bids needed to address interactivity and with my Computer Science Degree, I was an expert!

We bid successfully and gradually the company grew and won franchises for five London Boroughs and we renamed it Cable London.

But what I had not fully realised was it was all about digging up roads and getting wayleaves (right to dig) from Borough councils. This was an incredibly slow and frustrating process and although I had done very well from a pride perspective, it was not really giving me the fulfilment that I was looking for.

Moreover, because I had raised all that outside investment, my shareholding in the business was rapidly diminishing - I needed to find an additional business opportunity.

One evening I had just surfaced from a bath when a contact called me. Normally I would have asked Lesley to take a message, but something made me take the call, still dripping wet and towelled.

This guy informed me that the telephone information services run by British Telecom were being closed down. These provided cricket scores, weather forecasts, racing results etc.

British Telecom was looking for companies to take them over. They would be paid a small amount from the cost of each call. A new technology was born: Premium Rate Telephone Services.

Well, this set me alight because I realised there was one area that even British Telecom did not address and that was media interaction. I had the idea of joint venturing with newspapers to provide telephone horoscopes, competitions and racing results and radio and TV companies for competitions and voting.

I went to 3i who had already backed my cable TV franchise and were also involved in Windsor Television. I did a business plan with my accountant Melvin Kay, and 3i offered to back me. We founded Broadsystem and within a few months we were up and running in Camden Town and that was the vehicle that I wanted to use to found a heart-centred commercial business.

I had a meditation room in the offices specially built and I tried to foster a family atmosphere. At first, we had a lot of fun as the business took off rapidly. We were turning over a profitable £1m in just over a year and we succeeded in getting contracts from most of the newspapers and handling TV voting and small-scale competitions.

Also, I had a strange 'sign'. I'd always had a calling towards magic, real or imagined and news was reaching me about spoon bender Uri Geller. I was intrigued by his self-confidence and unconventional nature, which contrasted strongly with my own upbringing. Yet he was an Israeli Jew!

For the first time, it appeared possible to break free from my conditioning using him as a model.

Also, I wondered if Uri could predict stock market prices and I wrote to him about setting up a telephone service.

To my astonishment, he rang me back as soon as he received my letter and invited Lesley and me to meet him for tea at his fabulous house in Sonning. We arrived just as a party of handicapped kids had left. Uri is very quiet about the work he undertakes for charity, but he is one of the most generous people I have met both with his time and money.

Anyway, Uri did not feel comfortable with my stock market idea, but we became friends and we launched an even more outrageous idea. To remotely bend a spoon locked in a safe for a prize of £1m!

Believe it or not, we managed to insure against somebody achieving this feat!

We set up a whole registration system so we could track the success of entrants. But we need not have worried because nobody succeeded but we did receive massive publicity!

(www.urigeller.com/bend-spoon-win-1-million-offers-uri-geller)

People often ask if Uri is 'for real' or not. My answer has always been that I simply do not know. I have been half-expecting him to write some sort of 'confession' especially as he is now over 70 but I see no sign of it happening and he is always 'on message'.

Back at Broadsystem, news of the relative ease with which we were generating cash from premium rate calls got out and we began to be assailed by competitors who were offering crazy deals. We would split the revenue 50/50 with each client but 90/10 deals were available if you shopped around with our competitors.

Simultaneously we had to increase the number of employees in our organisation to handle the growing client base. Consequently, the family atmosphere that I had so sincerely wanted was lost very soon. We had to have managers at various levels because I could not keep an eye on every small detail – as much as I wanted to!

And we were losing business mainly because we simply would not take loss-making deals and I recognized that we would need to sell the company as our profit margins and cash dwindled.

Pretty soon my house was on the line. We lived in a time of negative equity, whereby mortgage repayments were fixed irrespective of interest rates in the market and the difference added to our debt. In short, our house was worth less than our outstanding mortgage. So, I needed to sell the house as soon as possible to keep myself afloat AND I needed to rescue the business.

Worse still, there was an ongoing Government enquiry into the future of premium rate telephone lines. We were threatened with closure.

As a consequence, I had attempted to diversify just in case we would no longer be able to trade in our core business and by some fluke, we had gained a contract to open a magazine with Granada Television in conjunction with their This Morning programme.

Looking back, it should have been possible to make a huge success of this but for us, it was a money-draining disaster.

You see I knew nothing about publishing and everything about telephone services!

Instead of following my intuition, I employed a team of publishing 'professionals,' who wanted to proceed traditionally with distribution through newsagents.

I wanted distribution by mail order, but they insisted this was not viable.

Also, I wanted the magazine to just feature items covered in the This Morning programme, but the team wanted to emulate Woman's Own, a popular magazine of the era.

And to make it even worse Granada insisted the magazine was weekly not monthly. I knew this wouldn't be viable for us unless it was an instant success – we simply didn't have enough money to support it.

But instead of pulling out or looking for a publishing partner, I blithely carried on. Luckily, I had set aside an amount for the venture and promised myself I would close the magazine if we spent that.

At least I had the presence of mind to stick to my guns, and we closed the magazine after eleven weeks. For the last edition, I insisted we simply cover features in the programme and have the presenters, Richard and Judy, on the cover. I knew it was too late to save the magazine but at least I could feel satisfied with the final edition.

Anyway, we plainly needed a miracle to save us and the business.

The TM Organisation could organize 'yagyas' (also known as yagnas) to bring better luck. A ceremony could be performed in an ashram in India to improve your life destiny.

As crazy as it seemed, I looked at the possibility of having a yagya undertaken to sell Broadsystem. I had £4,000 left in the bank, negative equity and the business was just about surviving.

I discussed the situation with Lesley and she agreed that we should spend our remaining £4,000 on the yagya.

The yagya was to last ten days. And if it didn't work, we would be fucked to use a technical term!

At that time, our largest client was the Daily Mirror newspaper and we ran telephone racing results for them.

On the first day of the yagya, we also launched an online telephone competition with them to win a car. We had won this business from a competitor who was extremely cross with us!

As the competition began, our computers mysteriously malfunctioned. Remember the yagya had just started and so this turn of events was not exactly what I had hoped for!

A staff member informed me that first thing in the morning a British Telecom van had entered our car park and a BT engineer was seen tampering with the wires to our computer. I put two and two together and here was my first example of sabotage. Within a few minutes, I had the Managing Editor of the Daily Mirror on the phone. He was livid because he was receiving complaints from readers who could not enter the competition.

He told me that he was going to terminate our contract and that would have cost us £3 million a year. There was nothing I could do other than to send my own engineers into the computer room to try and ascertain what had happened.

Then I sat under my desk and drank a cup of tea! I received odd glances from the staff, but they were used to my eccentricities by then.

I told Nina, my secretary, not to allow any disturbances while I sat there and attempted to come up with a strategy to resolve this particular crisis.

Despite my orders, Nina held out a phone and told me that the Managing Editor of The Times, Michael Hoy, was on the phone.

The Times was ultimately owned by Rupert Murdoch's News Corporation and we had a tiny telephone racing results service with The Times – which is how Michael knew me.

I expected him to give me a roasting, but he sounded calm enough and didn't seem to know that we were experiencing technical problems. I didn't confess…

To my astonishment, he asked if I'd like to sell my business to Rupert Murdoch!

I feigned nonchalance as my heart raced whilst he explained that a John Evans was in town from America and wanted to identify entrepreneurs who could work for Murdoch. Michael had kindly suggested me, and I was to meet John at the Stafford Hotel that very afternoon. I was rather stunned…

As I left for the meeting, our computer had been fixed and the telephone competition with the Daily Mirror was working as well as The Times Racing Results service.

The year was 1990, which was to turn out to be one of the most momentous of my life. At the beginning of that year I was to meet Robert Maxwell who owned the Daily Mirror, then Rupert Murdoch and finally Maharishi Mahesh Yogi.

The Robert Maxwell meeting had been arranged by my friend Colin Turner who seemed to know everyone at a high level. In this instance Ernie Burrington, then Managing Editor of the Mirror. There was no particular agenda, but I think Colin had suggested Broadsystem might be for sale and since the Mirror was our largest client, we would make a natural acquisition target.

Maxwell was larger than life in both physique and charisma and in his office stood a huge Alpine horn, which had been given to him by the Swiss Government as an honour.

I asked him to play the horn for me and he clambered on to his desk and started blowing. At which point Peter Jay, Maxwell's Chief of Staff appeared, looked at the astounding scene and hurried out again.

Maxwell did indeed offer to buy Broadsystem, but before things could progress very far Ernie rang to inform me that Maxwell's son was to acquire a competitor and therefore discussions could not proceed further.

I never heard more about the son's acquisition and the Daily Mirror business continued for another year.

But coming back to the meeting at the Stafford Hotel…

John Evans was an eccentric Welshman and was not that interested in what I actually did but seemed more fascinated by how my mind worked.

I later discovered that John had sailed to New York and passed out due to alcoholic excess and found himself staring at The Statue of Liberty without remembering how he got there!

He worked in the New York marina but gradually found his way into publishing with The Village Voice, perhaps the first alternative magazine, which was bought by Murdoch.

John and I chatted about life, the Universe and everything and at the end of the meeting said that he wanted me to meet 'Rupert' and he would be in touch again soon.

It was Friday - just a few days after the yagya had begun - and I went home and explained what had happened to Lesley.

To be honest, I didn't expect to hear more. The Evans meeting was so bizarre, I thought nothing could come of it but true to his word on Sunday evening John rang to tell me that Rupert wanted to meet me at 10 am the next morning at his Wapping headquarters.

There were demonstrations by the print unions outside Wapping at that time. And my taxi driver was very disparaging about Rupert Murdoch as many people were and I guess as many people still are. Anyway, I still couldn't believe what was happening.

I was escorted to a meeting room where Mr Murdoch and various members of his senior management sat.

And once again it was a surreal meeting where he asked me a little about my business and how much I wanted for it. I made up a realistic figure given our drop in our revenue. I had outside shareholders, one of whom would not be happy with the figure I suggested, but the others would be delighted.

Before the disgruntled shareholder would approve the deal, I had to promise to personally reimburse them for any potential loss of value in the shares they had bought a few months before the sale.

Remarkably, by the time the yagya had ended I had exchanged contracts with News Corporation and once again I was an employee - but at least I was not bankrupt and I used this experience to downsize and never again have I had a mortgage or any debt.

Before continuing it is worth describing how I met Maharishi because of those three meetings with remarkable men, this was equally, or perhaps even more, significant.

I received a message from David Lines who had been on my TM Teacher Training course and was now working in the TM Movement headquarters in The Netherlands, that Maharishi wanted to meet me to discuss a special project. Lesley and I were told to fly to Amsterdam, travel to a hotel near the headquarters and wait. It was a Sunday and I needed to be back in London for an important meeting the next day.

We waited and waited in our hotel room and after a couple of hours there was a knock at the door and we were told to get in a car which would drop us at the headquarters.

There we waited again. It was around 4 pm. The hours passed, nightfall came, and I was getting agitated because I really did not want to delay my return to London.

Just before midnight, we were invited to Maharishi's room. I was ushered to a seat in front of him and also there was a magician already seated, called Doug Henning.

Maharishi addressed us, saying that he wanted to set up a virtual reality theme park - remember this was 1990 - and Doug and I were to work together to establish it. Doug would also introduce me to a property developer who would arrange some land for the venture.

As he spoke a strange thing occurred. Despite what you may think by now, I'm rather sceptical by nature, but as I watched Maharishi, he appeared to become white light in front of my eyes. I kept blinking but he would appear alternately as his normal image or light.

The meeting was short and sweet, and we were returned to our hotel. Maharishi would continue his meetings and we heard that he had to be persuaded each night to rest - probably so his staff could sleep!

The next morning before our flight home, Doug and I met for a short while and I was given the contact details of the property developer whom I subsequently met. But nothing ever came of the project and I heard no more from Maharishi.

David Lines and I are still friends and David now teaches TM in California. David told me that Maharishi was often starting these projects, which seemed to go nowhere. Maybe there was something more mystical going on.

Rather poignantly Doug died shortly after our meeting...

Back to News Corporation... It has a chequered history, but they were always very good to me and working in a large corporation gave me many insights but rather corrupted my moral compass and eventually I had to leave. But during that particular journey, I realised a lot about what being authentic in business really meant.

The first couple of years with them were amazing.

No longer did I have to worry about cash and although I made very little myself out of the deal after I'd paid back the mortgage company and the disgruntled shareholder, Mr Murdoch had suggested I be put on a 10% profit share to keep me motivated. That and my considerable salary boosted our savings considerably.

I had always wanted to run a big competition with a TV company but that was not allowed in those days, because mass telephone promotions would have brought down the emergency telephone services and were prohibited by the Independent Broadcasting Authority.

I was introduced to Bruce Gyngell, Chief Executive of TV-AM by my friend Jeremy Fox. TV-AM was about to lose its breakfast television broadcasting licence and luckily he was based next door to my office in Camden Town.

I met Bruce one day during his morning trampoline workout. He was bouncing up and down dressed in shorts and he asked if there was any way I could generate significant sums of money for the TV-AM shareholders before the franchise closed.

I became very excited and told him that if he were to give away a car on-air, his company would make £1m. But first, he had to get permission from the Broadcasting Authority. And I had to get permission for this mass call-in competition from British Telecom (BT).

Bruce persuaded the Authority and luckily for me, BT had just upgraded their telephone network, so we obtained the go-ahead for the competition, which we ran for the company's closing four months. We were able to generate £997,000 for TV-AM which I rounded up to £1 million and we made the same. I became a hero at TV-AM and for many years after they ceased broadcasting I was invited to their reunions.

Then one Sunday morning after the acquisition I came into my London office and there was a fax appearing to come from Rupert Murdoch asking me if I would like to go to Boston with him as he was considering buying a relatively new Internet company there.

I thought it might be a joke, although it had to be a pretty sophisticated joke because the fax was on News Corporation headed notepaper.

I rang Murdoch's office the next day and his PA confirmed that indeed I was to go to New York to meet Mr Murdoch and he would take me on his private jet to Boston from New York.

This was all a fantasy to me as you can imagine but I travelled to New York, of course.

I was staying at The Gramercy Park Hotel, which was then an old-fashioned family-run hostelry and they had keys to the private Gramercy Park opposite.

I had arrived fairly late the night before but because of jet lag, I was up early, and I asked the doorman to let me into Gramercy Park for twenty minutes so I could get some fresh air and then let me out again. I was unshaven and had not showered.

I wandered around taking in the air and then presented myself back at the locked park entrance, but the doorman was nowhere to be seen and the clock was ticking.

New York in those days was not a particularly safe place so although I kept shouting out to passers-by to ask them to alert the doorman, nobody took any notice as they assumed that I was a tramp. But eventually, a kind soul summoned the doorman who came rushing over, incredibly embarrassed and released me.

I now only had 30 minutes to get to the meeting on time. I rushed to my room, showered, shaved and dressed, then hailed a cab. I arrived just as Mr Murdoch was exiting the lift of the News Corporation offices on Avenue of the Americas.

We travelled to Teterboro Airport in his limo with other senior executives and boarded his plane. The other guys examined me suspiciously. Who was this interloper? I suspected I was a threat to them in the feudal system that large organisations often become.

It was then that I realised that although this was all very good for my ego, the overriding imperative seemed to be to get as close to the boss as possible, whatever it took. This wasn't a game I wanted to play or that I played very well.

And as time went on, I became more frustrated. My company had a monopoly over all TV and newspaper telephone services in the Group, so financially I did extremely well but spiritually I was unfulfilled.

Then I made a big mistake. I was contracted to stay at News for three years but at the end of the three years the CEO of

News International, to whom I then reported, offered me a joint venture deal whereby I would own 30% of a new company where I would come up with all the ideas and they would bankroll the ones they liked. It was an offer too good to refuse - or so I thought.

But a few weeks after signing the deal that CEO was fired unceremoniously and any idea I suggested was blocked by his successors.

I was going crazy and paid a fortune to do nothing! It was the Electricity Council scenario yet again!

Luckily, I had become friends with Mr Murdoch's daughter Elisabeth, and I confided my woes to her.

A few days later she suggested we meet for a drink and unknown to me, asked her father to join us... Thanks to her I could unveil my idea for Sky Television to launch a phone service. Mr Murdoch kindly arranged a meeting of his executives and myself the next morning at Wapping and gave my idea the green light and that venture proceeded successfully.

But none of my other ideas (including a service which would have been like Skype - before Skype had been conceived) was given the go-ahead.

Then Fate intervened and I was diagnosed with colon cancer.

I'd had symptoms for three years but had ignored them and they were getting progressively worse.

I was a vegetarian and meditated and I had also gone to see some top Indian Ayurvedic doctors in Germany. They had examined me, taken my pulse, and told me there was nothing particularly wrong with me.

But then something spooky happened that saved my life.

In that German retreat centre with the Ayurvedic specialists was a group of psychics. I was eating my dinner alone and one of them came and sat opposite me uninvited. She told me that I was very ill, and I should get treatment immediately.·

Then, a few days later, I was having lunch with my friend Malcolm Gee, and he told me I looked ghastly and insisted I see a doctor.

Thanks to them I am alive today!

I finally got diagnosed but I had to completely revisit my beliefs as regards the degree to which an alternative lifestyle could protect me from serious illness.

I had a tremendous surgeon, Professor Dorudi who operated on me. It was a major operation and I lived, but it left me in a bit of a quandary because I knew that working for someone else was no longer good for me.

I resigned from News Corporation and they were very generous in the circumstances. Before my diagnosis, I had agreed to sell my 30% interest in the venture we had started together, but that would have been over three years.

However, they paid me what they owed me up-front.

I took a couple of years to recover. At first, I could barely walk upstairs to the bedroom. Then I managed 100 yards to the Coffee Cup café in Hampstead High St. Finally, I was able to walk across Hampstead Heath.

It was a time for introspection and reflection. I had enough money accumulated from my profit share and the sale of my shares in the joint venture, but I was at a loss as to what to do next.

I certainly did not want to start another business. I had experienced near bankruptcy, financial success and nearly died!

Going on in the same vein was not an option. Also, most people who have had a major illness look for reasons as to why. I had no idea, but I promised myself I would start again.

I gave up being an Orthodox Jew because I had become Agnostic and had been living a lie for several years. I had already resigned my job and then on a meditation retreat in Suffolk, I was to meet Luiza who was to become my second wife following an amicable divorce from Lesley.

Gradually I was asked to sit on the boards of different companies with various degrees of satisfaction, and I tried where I could to bring in fair and generous practices.

I was very honoured to be asked by Elisabeth Murdoch to join the Board of her fledgling Shine television production company and we worked together until her business was sold.

I did other gigs in technology, the worst of which was Chairman of a public company in the Alternative Investment Market (AIM). There I had to learn what happens when you have a company that is not doing very well and has thousands of small shareholders.

Around three years ago, I decided to step back from the business and devote myself to helping other people through mentoring.

I say to people, I am retired. Luiza says I will never retire, and who knows what the future will be. I am offering you this book and these interviews to help you decide whether you want to become an entrepreneur, what it actually means to be one, how I think you can succeed, and to guide you along the way.

Part 2: The Interviews

1

Paul Boross

Inspirational Speaker, Comedian, Psychologist,
Humourologist, The Pitch Doctor

www.bigsky.me

I first met Paul on a meditation retreat at least 30 years ago. I'm not sure what he was doing there because he has never talked about it since, but we got on immediately and stayed in touch.

He kindly spent some time with me using his executive coaching skills to wheedle out what I wanted to do with my life before we came up with the idea of this book.

As you can see from his eyes, he is one of the kindest people I know. Apart from being a renaissance man - Keynote Speaker, Comedian, Musician, international executive coach, psychologist, charity mentor and TV Personality.

I admire him immensely, although in some respects we could not be more different. Whereas I am rather a hermit and would be quite happy meditating for days on end, he is always up to something. Performing one night, off to some conference the next.

Let Paul tell you himself...

My calling was for showing off, really!

My first clear memory may sound bizarre. I was in my first year at primary school and the nativity play was in casting and I had a desperate urge to be cast as the lead, Joseph.

I remember frequently reminding my primary school teacher that I could do that and wanting to do it. I think a lot of these things are inherent feelings.

But the trouble is that when people get older, they stop trusting their gut instinct and their feelings.

Throughout my life, I've always gone back to those feelings and asked, 'what do I really want?' And I think I've just become very good at trusting my heart and not my head and therefore haven't been side-tracked by the 'sensible thing'. And I've always gone for what my parents would have described as the silly option!

My father was a Hungarian refugee. He was 30 when he arrived here and he had to work for two years as a waiter before he could go back into his profession, which was economics.

My father was desperate for me not to go near anything to do with show business or acting because as he would frequently remind me, 95% of people in those kinds of businesses are out of work at any one time.

And similar to other successful entrepreneurs that I've met, I think once you have a passion and once you have a purpose, successful people just keep going for it despite what those around say. And despite people trying to take you off-track.

People are constantly trying to make you more like them, make you conform, put you in a specific box. And I think I'm just bloody-minded enough not to want to do what other people do. And also prepared to put up with the difficulties of walking a different path because people don't particularly like it when you step outside the norm.

They may try and bring you back into something they understand. They'll use all manner of things to bring you back. And that could be, what we colloquially call 'taking the piss'. It could be belittling. Perhaps when you have a failure or perceived failure, they will jump on that.

I think the path of an entrepreneur or in my case an entertainment entrepreneur, is made more difficult because I think people inherently feel they want to do what you're doing, but they are fearful of doing it and don't actually like you showing them up by doing it.

If you look at the creative industries, people are desperate to get in there, so it's even harder.

I should also stress that it was only about 10 years ago that my mother stopped cutting job adverts out of the paper and sending them to me.

She'd say, 'Why don't you get a franchise, you would be really good and it's easy'.

I would go, 'Mother, have we met, do you know who I am and what I do?'

She'd reply, 'No, I'm just trying to be helpful because what you do is so very difficult'.

When you become a parent you realise that parents just want to protect you.

They just didn't want me to be unhappy or insecure because doing those things equated in their minds to poverty. And no parent wants their child to go through hardship.

So, if you go an individual path, you're fighting against stepping out of the norm.

I think you have to be very singular. You have to be sometimes foolishly confident in your own ability and you have to have that ability to constantly bounce back from adversity. And some people don't want to get up off the canvas that many times. The Chinese say success is being knocked out six times but getting up seven!

Stephen: What I've noticed about your life is that you seem to have built up a community of like-minded people as your friends as you've met them through your journey.

Paul: I value friendship so much above everything else.

When you take a different path, you need a support structure and supportive people, positive people.

You also need to learn from those people.

I always made sure that I stayed friends with people as much as possible. Even old girlfriends.

But I'm no saint. I've been through fallings out with people.

In those instances, I've written letters apologising even though I don't know what I've done but there are times when you just can't work out what happened.

It could be that the other person is going through something you don't understand. And it may be something to do with you, but it may be nothing to do with you. Maybe that you anchor a memory in their mind, or it makes them feel awkward or they've gone so far down that line, they find it difficult to come back.

Authenticity is, if you feel something, you must act on it even though there are all kinds of different emotions involved.

I was listening to Sadiq Khan, Mayor of London on the radio. He said, 'Since I've been on this radio programme, I've actually made three mistakes about what I've said, and I'd like to correct these things'.

I think that's what authenticity is because everybody makes mistakes.

He continued explaining that the problem is that our current Government won't admit they've made a mistake, yet people will forgive anybody for making a mistake because there isn't anybody who hasn't.

I think one of the hardest things, from a psychological stance, is to admit your mistakes because if you go on not taking responsibility it reaches a tipping point and that's when disaster strikes.

Stephen: You've dealt with many entrepreneurs. What are the main characteristics of those who have been successful? Not necessarily in becoming billionaires, but just having a fulfilled life. And what lessons can you pass on to other people that want to be happy as well as having enough money to live on?

Paul: I've worked with hugely successful entrepreneurs, billionaires and top CEOs but the ones I think have the balance right are the ones who value humour. Humour, I think, is the differentiator. I'm writing a book called Humourology - The Serious Business of Comedy at Work. It is essentially about how humour can dramatically improve your business success and your life.

People who are really authentic are the ones who connect with other people and the greatest shortcut to connecting with people is humour.

It was the Dutch comedian Victor Borge who said, 'a smile is the shortest distance between two people'.

If you have humour, a lightness of touch in your business, you are going to create a whole feeling in the organisation.

As my mother would say, 'You get more with sugar than vinegar'.

When people are putting adverts now on the internet to find love, the number one thing they seem to require is a 'good sense of humour' because that's compelling to everyone.

Where do happiness and fulfilment come from?

Do they come when you open your computer to view your banking records and your profits or is it when you gather your team together and you laugh together and celebrate together and have joy together?

HR people talk about retention. How do you do that? They say, 'Let's give them more money'. Well, that actually doesn't drive retention.

What drives retention is people feeling good. So actually, if you are going to be an Authentic Entrepreneur, you better learn how to make people feel good. Make them smile, make them laugh. Share that moment of lightness, of laughter.

My friend David McCourt is a billionaire and he said something that really resonates with me, 'What people don't realise is that a lot of people are not just interested in money, they will do a deal just because they like you or want to help you'.

Bring some fun into people's lives.

Learn to 'anchor' people into a state whereby when they see you, they think 'This'll be fun!'.

Stephen: I come from a generation where nobody was encouraged to be an entrepreneur but now it seems to be the opposite! If somebody wasn't sure, but all their peers were setting up on their own, what would you say?

Paul: I would actively argue with them!

I'd say, 'I really don't think you want to do this' and I would push them until, hopefully, they started to fight back, get passionate and argue for themselves. I would just keep going until I make them get more and more angry and belligerent about the fact that they do want to be an entrepreneur.

As someone who has executive coached people at the highest level, I know what it takes to succeed so I always need to be convinced that they actually do want to do it.

The fact is, if you are not completely passionate and focused on being an entrepreneur, you won't succeed.

Any entrepreneur must have that inherent enthusiasm and passion whereby they would do it anyway, even if there wasn't this pot of gold at the end of the rainbow. Because it's not the easy route. You have to be prepared to work much harder than somebody working in an office in a regular job.

You can give yourself three things that you want to do and then give yourself a timeline and actually reach those goals.

Just three things.

And at the end of the month, you go, 'Yes, I've done all those things'. Then you have to multiply it by 10 and go, 'Can I do that every week, week in, week out, month in, month out, year in, year out and self-start all the time'.

Because if you don't feel that you can do that, being an entrepreneur is not for you.

The bravest people are the ones who understand that it's not for them.

But true entrepreneurs should get into a habit of creating things and committing to their goals.

Start with one thing. Be somebody who does things.

From a psychological perspective, if you're going to be an entrepreneur, you'd better understand yourself. Learn all the things that went well.

'I committed to that. I did that. I committed to that. I did that'.

I don't care how many of them worked, but you have to see things through. Some things you will realise halfway through are not going to work.

My advice is to become one of those people who understand how goals work, how seeing things through works and you have to know what your outcome is. You also have to put things on a timeline and learn about reverse engineering. Understand how to put things on a timeline and go stage by stage.

I've got no time for people who say 'I am a great entrepreneur and one day I am going to do...'.

It's not about that. It's about little victories along the way.

It's a task thing. And as you become a bigger entrepreneur, your tasks become bigger, your goals become bigger.

The success is in doing. In short, I'm saying become a doer.

Paul has always been an inspiration to me in his positivity, creativity, humour and passion.

He first suggested the idea of this book and to be brave enough to describe my life, with all its idiosyncrasies to you readers.

Several times I have felt like giving up because writing, and then editing require significant focus but a chat with Paul would inspire me to keep on going on and for that, I owe him a huge vote of thanks!

2

Gaelle Kennedy

Founder, Gaelle Organic

www.gaelleorganic.com

We had the good fortune to bump into Gaelle on one of our walks in Ojai, California where we have been spending our winters.

One of the benefits of stepping away from being full-time and taking on Non-Executive Directorships is that they allow travelling for longer periods whilst being able to give advice and mentorship and provide a modest income.

Normally Board meetings are held monthly and used to require personal attendance, but in these post-pandemic days, that is less of an issue. We originally found Ojai because I was on the Board of The Ink Factory film company and one of its founders, Stephen Cornwell, lives in Ojai and suggested we spend our winters there, especially as the company had offices in both London and LA, only a short drive away and where I could attend meetings as necessary.

We fell in love with the place and community and have kept returning for the past years.

Ojai was the setting for Shangri-La in the film Lost Horizon where the inhabitants aged much slower than in the outside world and 'coincidentally' Gaelle is an excellent example of how it is possible to look young and vibrant at any age.

Now for the interview…

I was born in a Displaced Persons Camp at the end of the War. My parents were Holocaust survivors and in this DP camp, which was in Landsburgh, Germany, I was the first Jewish born child in 1946.

My recollection of that time was actually very happy. I remember going on picnics with my parents and so forth. Then we emigrated to the United States pretty much like stowaways, because we were supposed to go to Palestine, but they wouldn't let anybody go who was not well or had an infection because it was a treacherous trip.

I had scratched my smallpox vaccination and therefore was disqualified. And my father had only a brother who survived out of 10 children and he went to Palestine and we were supposed to go with him. And what's interesting in this story is how our lives are shaped by things we have no understanding of at that moment.

Especially now I'm 74 years old and I spend a lot of time reflecting on my life and how did I get here?

So, we couldn't go to Palestine and wound up going to America and that was in itself something that was beyond what my parents wanted. That was part of my soul journey because I wasn't supposed to go to Palestine at that time.

In America, it was a very difficult childhood. I was discriminated against. First of all, I was very blonde, blue eyes and I looked very German so the Jews were against me because they didn't know I was Jewish and they thought I was a Nazi because I only spoke German and Polish. I had no friends, and nobody wanted to play with me. I was kind of an outcast and relied on my creativity and imagination.

And that's what gets me through my life today.

My parents sent me to Israel when I was 17 because my father's family all lived in Jerusalem. I went there and felt an immediate spiritual, soulful connection to the country.

I travelled between New York and Israel and couldn't make up my mind which country I wanted to live in.

I worked as a model in New York but because I didn't have the height - I was only five, five and you had to be at least five, seven - I was limited in what I could do.

But in Israel, the criteria for models was not to be that tall, so I got very fortunate. I had a great agent and I became one of the top models in Israel and internationally.

I had acne, which is very common for young women and I'd always had to put all this makeup on my face and chest.

I taught myself about makeup and how to cover up when I broke out.

One day Der Spiegel magazine came to Israel for a feature which was to be called The Three Beauties of Israel and I was chosen as one of them.

We went to the Dead Sea and I covered myself up, including my chest, because I had acne breakouts. All of a sudden, the water wiped off all the makeup on my chest and I said to Hava, who was Miss Israel, 'Oh my God, all these pimples, what am I going to do?'

Within five minutes, those pimples disappeared because of the salt. And that was my first clue about what nature can do, especially to the skin.

I was so self-conscious because I was a leading model.

That experience triggered something in me. I wanted to learn everything at that early age about what nature could do to the skin.

I had never been in business. I knew nothing about business. I had no interest in business and quite frankly it all gives me a headache! Don't get me wrong, I love money, you know? But if I have to sit there and figure things out, I'd probably starve to death. I just don't have the patience!

Anyway, when my daughter was a teenager, she would bring home cosmetics from the shops.

I had told her it was really important what you put on your skin because it gets absorbed into your bloodstream. You should use organic products.

She was a teenager and rebellious. We'd get into fights because of all the junk that she brought home that she saw in magazines. That's how magazines get you. They spend a fortune on advertising promising you eternal youth and perfect skin. Beautiful pictures and a young gorgeous model.

My daughter said 'Seeing as you know so much, why don't you make your own creams?'

Bingo.

I started to play with things. I had a lot of years' experience about what works, what doesn't. First of all, you've got to clean your skin and then if you have large pores you need to learn how to tighten them naturally. So, I started doing research and seeing what each ingredient does. And I thought I'm going to make the best cream that anybody's ever used.

And it was just an idea to show what I know.

Then 2008 hit and we were living in this beautiful home and for three years we couldn't sell it and everything that could go wrong economically went wrong for us. Another phase of life.

One day I was walking, and I remember the tree I was under when I got this epiphany of an ingredient that I thought to try in my cream. The whole idea was just to have one great cream, a moisturizer, nothing else. It was going to be organic.

And I thought, 'I'm going to call it Gaelle Organic. Why not?'

I made the cream. I got to know a woman who really understood how you make creams, how you know what you need and it's complex.

She lived in Washington and she became my mentor. She was very into organics and Paul, my husband, and I flew down to meet her and learn everything we could.

She had all these herbs. She was making them in jars and it excited me. That part of it, the formulation really is exciting to me because I love putting things together and seeing what it does and then trying it. Now that I'm at the ripe age of 74, I know what works and what doesn't.

I started with four products and we had this packaging, which I thought was very lovely.

I was selling maybe four or five creams a month. That was it. And everybody came back and said it was the best cream they'd ever had.

Things started growing like that.

I wanted to be bigger than just selling to my friends and I knew two shops that are important because everybody buys there. One was in Beverly Hills and one was in Los Angeles and they catered to all the actresses, the studios.

I knew if I could make it there, I had something good. I was there every weekend standing on my feet demonstrating and talking. I'm very good one on one and I can look at them and help them.

I said, 'Listen, it's 50% what you eat and 50%, what you feed your skin'.

I would teach them to read the ingredients. Nobody reads ingredients. When you eat, you read ingredients. Why wouldn't you read ingredients on cosmetics?

Then a make-up artist wrote an article that I had the best skincare. Remember I only had four products then. But he spread the word in New York.

Then I met hairdresser Cim Mahoney and he's Danish and he and his wife wanted to sell it in Denmark. The lovely thing for me about business is when you meet people and you become friends, that's the best. We've been friends now for eight or nine years, really good friends.

They helped me change my packaging. Gaelle Organic has to stand out. I said, 'I care about ingredients. This is what I'm preaching. See what you're putting on your face'.

But they insisted on better packaging and we still have the same packaging today.

People are getting more educated and the green organic world is opening up and it's become a billion-dollar business.

I'd like to be in that business, you know, to get that kind of success. I would do things differently with that money. I wouldn't need a McMansion. I would secure myself so I wouldn't have to worry, because we're not there yet. We still have to worry about paying the bills and we have a few people working for us. So, I'd like to have a little lovely house in nature. Something small, nothing big. And then start charitable organisations.

To encourage young people to be creative and to think.

I have a very good friend who became a rabbi and she said that the first question God asks you is, 'How were you in business?' (see www.aish.com/ci/be/The-Talmudic-Formula-for-Success.html).

Business is spiritual because we all need to eat. We all need to take care of families. And when you lie, when you cheat someone, you are denying them of their right to do the same.

And basically, you're creating bad karma.

I'm very proud of our business. We're candid, open, honest. Often, we say, 'No, my cream isn't for you. You've big pores. And when you have big pores, you don't use a moisturizer!'

And people get shocked that I tell them not to buy the cream. It's not for them.

We now have 2000 customers and Paul actually runs the business. He runs the whole thing. I stick with the creams; I stick with talking to the clients when they have a question. And that's the part I enjoy. The other part I don't understand. I don't enjoy it and I don't do it. So that's it. We have a very simple 30 days money back policy.

A woman with a turkey neck asked what cream she should use. I told her no cream could fix it. They have masks which pull your skin. I said, 'If you're going to tighten your skin, get an organic plastic surgeon. I have two names. Go see them'.

I won't sell anybody anything that I don't think is going to work for them.

The Authentic Entrepreneur

In conclusion, I'd tell budding entrepreneurs to make sure you love what you're doing and make sure you educate yourself well and are willing to work hard.

Following the pandemic, online is the future. It offers whole new opportunities.

We're going to be spending more time at home. I think this is a permanent game-changer. Some good things are going to come out of this!

Gaelle proves beyond a shadow of a doubt that age is no barrier to starting a business and providing you have someone with financial acumen working with you (in this case her husband Paul) you can build a successful business.

I loved the way she mentions that she doesn't want to go anywhere near the numbers but her passion is simply making and selling organic cosmetics to her growing customer base.

She also realises that being good to customers creates good karma which radiates out into society. We're all connected and Gaelle does her bit to spread fun, fairness and optimism.

3

Toby Clarke

Founder, Walking Ibiza

www.walkingIbiza.com

Luiza and I have spent the last 20 years travelling the world in our perpetual search for 'Paradise'. A place where we can spend some of the year with good weather and amongst like-minded community.

A place where Luiza can teach Qi Gong and meditation and I can amuse people. All between extended periods of silence.

We started far afield. Beginning with winters in India due to our mutual interest in meditation and Indian philosophy. India is a fascinating place but extremely hard work.

Luiza studied yoga with B. K. S. Iyengar in Pune and I visited her at the end of her course, and we made the first of our joint trips.

On one of our last trips to India, our train to visit a well-known astrologer in Kanpur (one of the most polluted cities in the world) was cancelled at the last minute and the next was not scheduled to leave for a week! A resourceful taxi driver offered to drive us there overnight and we reluctantly agreed.

We both dozed at the back of the cab and in the middle of the night, I woke, looked ahead, and saw 3 lanes of trucks heading towards us. Our driver had fallen asleep at the wheel, there were major roadworks, and he had ended up on the wrong carriageway. I screamed, and the driver pulled us over to a layby fortunately left by the highway contractors.

Being great believers in 'signs', we rapidly concluded India had no future for us or more precisely we might not have a future in India!

We continued our search closer to home and eventually, and at first rather reluctantly, found ourselves in Ibiza.

Reluctant because Ibiza has a certain reputation but Luiza and I don't frequent night clubs, don't take drugs and are normally in bed by 10 pm!

However, we did find a wonderful year-round community and we have been visiting off-season ever since.

Ibiza is beautiful, with secret coves, wonderful people and a spiritual vibe and one of our highlights are the walks organized by Toby Clarke's company Walking Ibiza although I have to confess that we normally join one led by Toby's mum Sheila, because it ends with tea and cake!

Sheila suggested I talk to Toby about Walking Ibiza and his particular 'trek' into business.

I spoke to Toby during the Ibiza Lockdown about his life, the formation of his business and his plans for the future and was struck by the number of parallels with my journey.

Over to Toby...

I was working for a company in England as Managing Director but had no shares.

We had started the company from scratch and picked up £2m in sales and I was thinking I can work for this company until I'm 75, probably get a good pension and retire happily and do some gardening. But I always wanted to do more. It just wasn't enough for me to be working for someone else and it was getting routine. I'd see the same clients every week.

So, I went to see the owner and in my jacket pocket, I hid my notice already written out, because I knew what the answer was going to be.

I asked for shares. I'd put all my heart into the company and none of it was mine. And he flatly refused.

'No, we never give any shares to anyone else outside of our family'.

Then I handed in my notice.

I had a six-month notice period, but I worked through it and then Belinda, my wife and I had to decide what we were going to do. We had a big house in the UK, and we lived this very lavish lifestyle. But we wanted to leave England and go and travel. Neither of us had travelled much before so we decided to get rid of everything and go backpacking.

We literally went from expense accounts and a big salary to travelling on $10 a day!

Initially, we wanted to go for two years. We travelled around Central and Southern America all the way down to the tip of Argentina, then back up to Peru.

We were in Cusco where we started hearing about shamans and we were expecting to find someone with long hair living in the jungle, whom we might not be able to understand. But we ended up doing this week-long immersion with Shaman Lilo from Switzerland!

One day, Belinda and I were about a hundred metres apart on top of a sacred mountain.

Whether you call it a download or God speaking or Buddha or Mohammed, whatever it might be, I thought 'I've got to go and tell Belinda'.

But Belinda was already walking towards me and we both said,

'I need to tell you something. We need to go to Ibiza now'.

So, three or four weeks later, we were on Ibiza, but we had no plans at all.

I was originally born on Ibiza. My mum Sheila was here between '69 and '79 and I was born in '70 and had the most amazing childhood before being taken to the UK when I was nine years old. But I always had this massive draw back to Ibiza.

We stayed with an old school teacher who loved nature and he showed us a few paths that he knew. I didn't really know what I wanted to do, but Belinda had learnt Reiki, a healing modality.

We started giving Reiki treatments together, which we called the Double Whammy, because you'd be receiving both male and female energies and we had some incredible experiences. I don't want to say we cured people with cancer, but we had people coming to us with horrible things and they would go away, cured.

But I was wanting something a bit more and that was why I came up with the idea of walking around the Island!

That was another strange moment.

I remember the exact place it happened in Ibiza Town. I had just ordered a cold beer and was looking out over the Marina.

Then the same thing happened as on the sacred mountain. I had this download, and it said 'Walk around the Island'.

This was in 2010 and I went on Google and typed 'coastal paths of Ibiza', but I searched and searched but nothing came up. And from what I could see, no one had ever walked around the coastline before although I've since found out people have done it.

It was the beginning of October, so I needed to do it quickly before the winter kicked in and the clocks changed.

The next morning, I woke up and something made me open up my drawer and throw in my wallet with all my money and credit cards.

I closed the drawer and there was the sound of a coin spinning round inside. I reopened the drawer and there was a one Euro coin. And I knew that I was supposed to walk around the Island with just one Euro!

Belinda said, 'Maybe just take enough food and water for 24 hours for you and Cosmo, our dog'.

So, I took a bag of dog biscuits for Cosmo and some food and two litres of water and started walking.

I was walking around Ibiza with no money and every single person gave me something apart from one bar, which is actually the richest bar on the whole of the Island!

I thought 'I've just met one of the richest men on the Island and he won't even give me a glass of water'.

But on the flip side, some of the simplest beach shacks would sit me down, give me the menu and say, 'Have anything you want and order something for your dog'.

That walk took 11 days and at the end, The Sunday Times published 'Guy Walks around Ibiza with one Euro. Left his job in the city and gone to find himself in Ibiza'. My 15 minutes of fame!

Then I met someone at a New Year's Eve Party in 2010 who didn't believe I'd walked around the island, yet he asked me to take him and his friends on a walk, in return for a free lunch.

They loved the walk and one of them persuaded me to set up a Facebook Event and that's how Walking Ibiza came about.

I would just publicise when I was taking Cosmo for a walk, but I could see how much people were getting out of it and I loved doing it.

Then someone rang me up and asked me to take his group on a walk for a fee.

My jaw dropped and I thought 'People would give me money to go on a walk?!'

That was a big revelation. So, I took these guys walking and they gave me a hundred or fifty Euros, which was quite a nice bit of money to come back with just for going for a walk with my dog and sharing my knowledge.

Then someone on one of the Friday walks came up and shoved money in my pocket and I asked what it was for? And they said, 'Well, you're sharing your knowledge and there should be an energy exchange'.

And again, I was amazed.

The same guy bought a hat on the next walk and asked for donations. Everyone started putting money in the hat and then I knew that there was a business there.

So that's how it progressed from those very first walks back in 2011 to doing what I'm doing now.

Last year, I walked with about 8,000 people.

Every week we do four different walks. My Mum does one called Short and Sweet, which is a shorter walk because of the tea and cake at the end.

On Fridays, we have the classic walk. On Mondays and Sundays, a social and Wednesdays, a Mindful Walk. I also branched out into kayaking on Wednesdays and Sundays from the beach at San Miguel.

Then I started Ibiza Food Tours.

I love food, love the odd drink, love walking. So, I thought why don't we combine the whole lot together. In Ibiza Town we stop at different locations; really obscure ones you wouldn't normally find. Hidden bars and tea shops and we go to the oldest bakery in town.

There's a rich variety of food here. The Arabs were here long ago and before that the Romans and now the Christians and everyone's brought their own food.

We get to meet the owners. Some of them have been here for 50, 60 years, doing the same thing every day.

Stephen: Your Mum speaks very highly of your business ethics and she relays various stories about how kind you are to the staff and how well you pay them compared to other people on the Island, how you have regular meetings, training meetings, and then you'll take them out for a meal. Can I ask you about that?

Toby: Tony Robbin's courses are the reason why I now lead the life I lead.

I probably wouldn't be on Ibiza otherwise. He gave us a very nice grounding in work ethics and how to treat people and how to understand them as well. When I was working in England, we implemented a lot of ideas to embrace the staff, which I use with Walking Ibiza.

At the beginning, I was doing everything myself because I was a one-man band and it nearly killed me! I was walking so much it gave me a herniated disc.

Then I thought I either come to a size where I'm comfortable walking once a day and that's all I do, or I need to get other people on board.

I wanted to grow bigger, so I needed other people, but also the right type of person because it takes a certain type to be a guide. Without them, Walking Ibiza would only be me!

To me, a company is the people. You've got to treat your staff well. I believe that if the company is making money, everyone should make money. I make more money than the rest of the staff, but I pay them fairly for each walk.

But then I expect a lot in return as well. Every new guide receives training, but after that, they can make the walk their own style.

Without staff, the company isn't anything and you've got to give them the freedom to do what they want to do and give them good remuneration.

Stephen: Do you have a vision of where you want to take your business, or do you just take it as it comes?

Toby: What do I want to do with Walking Ibiza?

There are a lot of possibilities. Do I franchise it, take it elsewhere? I do Around the Island walks on Formentera and Minorca, but do I keep making it bigger and bigger and bigger?

There's a limited supply of clients on Ibiza, so I could start doing it in other places, but at the end of the day, I don't feel like I want it to become this crazy big company.

I really like the idea that people still talk to me. I sit and answer emails and I love that.

It's a family business as well. My Mum works for me as well as Belinda. Sometimes my daughters help me, and I love that family feeling.

I'm making an okay living and I'm happy being as I am. At the end of the day, why work very much harder? Potentially I could be earning 10 times as much, but then I would probably have ten times less time to enjoy.

If I sat in front of the computer all day, I'd go mad. I'm trying to get the balance right.

I believe that to earn a good living you shouldn't have to work hard all the time and money should come to you without working crazy hours.

The belief that you work hard and draw a pension at 65 was my dad's belief, not mine. Then I had that big dawning, 'Oh my God, I'm living my life because it was my Dad's belief!'

That changed my mindset and when I gave up everything in England, my dad struggled with it massively. That's what made me realise it's got to be my life and not my dad's any more.

Stephen: Do you have any parting words for those people if they're not sure what they should be doing?

Toby: Make sure it's something you enjoy doing. Don't take on a company or start a franchise or whatever, unless you're really, really, passionate about it.

Many people dream about owning a cafe or shop then they are tied to that business. Remember if it's your business, you can't just go out for an afternoon because you've got to be in

The Authentic Entrepreneur

the shop, running it. So really make sure that what you intend to do gives you the freedom you desire.

And it can be a lot of very hard work at the beginning, although it never feels like hard work if you've chosen the right thing.

For me, trust is a massive word. You can talk to other people, but don't talk to other people too much. Because if you've got an idea and you are trusting yourself, it probably is great.

And don't listen to everyone else all the time. Take advice, but then you've got to make your own decision.

Toby exemplifies the perfect example of someone who follows their passion and allows it to guide them along to a fulfilling life.

He shows that if we can stop forcing and relax into uncertainty, the easier our journey can become.

He is being paid to do exactly what he would have done anyway, shares the rewards with his guides, brings his family into the business and along the way turns clients into friends.

4

Aron Hughes

Founder, Sun And Sage Clothing

www.sunandsageclothing.com

Aron Hughes was suggested by our friend, Heidemarie Riedel, who like Aron is a passionate vegan but what really sparked my interest was the fact that Aron, although British, is living in Bali.

On the final India exploration that Luiza and I undertook, we were in Pondicherry, which was formerly a French colony where police still dress in the traditional French-style uniform, making the whole place quite quaint and charming.

On the edge of Pondicherry is the spiritual community of Auroville established by the Indian sage Sri Aurobindo and his paramour The Mother, whose real name was Mira Alfassa. You can read about it at www.auroville.org.

Well without going into details, it wasn't for us because, as with most communities, there were tensions which seem to go hand in hand with the human condition.

So, we were sitting rather despondently in a café, when out of nowhere came the realisation that I had a distant friend, Peter Wrycza, from my early TM days who now runs a retreat centre in Bali. Goodness knows where these thoughts spring from, but a few minutes later I was emailing him and arranging a visit and we ended up visiting, leasing a house for 5 years and Luiza teaching at a large yoga studio.

Our house was up a long winding road which was delightful during the day. The Balinese are very welcoming and have long memories and so every year everyone would remember us and welcome us back.

But at night, the road was ruled by packs of stray, aggressive dogs who would block our path and jump at us. No fun at the best of times, especially as rabies was sometimes prevalent.

This whole situation was mysterious. The Balinese theoretically worship dogs so it seemed strange that this situation should persist.

A local ex-pat explained his Dog Survival Strategy. You simply buy a big umbrella, wave it above your head and scream at the pack. This actually worked, but we mainly resorted to using local cabs and eventually our own car to drive in and out of Town at night!

Our time in Bali came to an end after 'investing' in a business without realising that as transient visitors we couldn't own shares or property and we were not prepared to take up residency.

The lesson being Do Due Diligence, especially if you are looking at a business in an overseas territory.

Bali is a magical place, filled with the wonderful, beaming Balinese and dreamy ex-pats. One can have all the trappings of a Western life with a fraction of the cost. But, as with any location, one must be aware of the pitfalls.

I was intrigued to interview Aron Hughes, whose passion for saving animals, veganism and improving the connection between his customers and his businesses shines through.

Over to Aron…

I've worked in the charity world all my life but in about 2012, I was really struggling to find a job in the UK. There was always, 'somebody with a bit more experience'.

Then I was offered an initial six-month contract at the Bali Animal Welfare Association, which is a local dog and cat rescue organisation. Animal welfare is very close to my heart and I ended up being there 8 years.

I was working part-time and rescuing street animals in my spare time but struggling to pay for it all.

Then I thought maybe if I can create an ethical business that links the two passions in my life, veganism and rescuing animals, hopefully, I can give other people ways to connect the two.

I'd been a vegan for a while, but I wasn't as passionate as I used to be. But seeing all these other new passionate people out there really sparked the fire in me. So, in 2017 I launched Sun and Sage Ethical Vegan Clothing.

It started with just a couple of t-shirts and selling to a few friends and then it snowballed from there.

I have another job at the moment, which is working with the Bali Children's Project. I work with them from nine to five doing appeals, donor development, making sure that we're sponsoring children at school. And I'm very passionate about that as well.

But in my business, things are definitely going in the right direction. I've learnt a lot more about how to market myself. If you check out my website, the whole marketing behind it is that you're supporting a real guy and none of it is fake.

I go to markets and take an animal in if it looks like it's really in trouble. Just showing people what the ethical side of the business really, truly is and that you don't necessarily have to go and buy from a big high street chain.

You can purchase from a smaller business that's doing good things for the world and gets you as good or better product.

It's started to grow as my marketing has improved and there's been a growing amount of word of mouth recommendations.

I'm slowly growing the product range so I can reinvest into purchasing new products. Now I've got kids t-shirts too and some sticker packs. I didn't make any profit until this year. It's still pretty low and I still use a good portion of it on animal rescue but it's going in the right direction.

Stephen: Have you considered bringing in outside investors?

Aron: I haven't looked into that. So far, I've looked at ways I can do it myself.

But I do need to look at other things. My marketing budget, for example, is pretty much non-existent and relies on word of mouth and social media. But if that were removed then I'd really struggle. But so far, I haven't progressed any investment opportunities.

Stephen: Do you have any mentors?

Aron: Well, my wife is a huge, huge support for me and she's behind me in whatever I do.

When I come home with a scabby animal or when I've got two ideas, she's a bit of a bouncing board. She's always supported me from the very start.

And my family is a really good source of support too. Sales don't always get sent from Indonesia unless it makes financial and environmental sense. So, in most cases, they get sent from the UK. And at the moment my stock in the UK is with my dad!

He's slowing down and retiring a little bit more so he's got the time and he really wanted to help and I've seen a lot more interest from the people around me.

They're saying, 'Oh, I thought you'd have given up by now'. Then they're being pleasantly surprised that I'm still going and still doing okay with it.

Stephen: What's it like doing business in Indonesia?

Aron: This is my only real experience of running my own business. The truth is I really don't know what it would be like running a business in the UK. But there are some really good points about working here.

I can walk into the production and say hello to everyone, they're smiling back at me, they're enjoying their jobs and I have traceability of how I'm producing my products.

It's really good for an entrepreneur here because you're not paying massive rates for everything. You're also able to access well-made good products by people who are paid fairly, but it still works as a great deal for you.

Stephen: What would you share with anybody wanting to get into business for the first time themselves? What's the best advice you could give them?

Aron: On the days when you're not selling anything, you feel like nobody cares about you and you're on your own. Of course, you'll always have friends and family to support you.

If you've got faith and confidence in your product and what you're doing and you know people will love it, then really, it's just a case of getting it in front of your client base. Hopefully, you can do a lot better than you thought in the first place.

I'm not there yet either, but I've got really good hopes about how things have gone.

It makes me very happy. It's my hobby as well. I love being able to show that there's the ethical side of this and there are all sorts of different connections that people can make.

Maybe they'll see that the t-shirt's all vegan made and then be wondering what's that about?

I think ethical business can really help change mindsets. When you buy mass-produced items it's easy to forget how they're made and what the ethical or unethical side of their production might be.

Aron exemplifies how, when young and without responsibilities, you can take a leap into the unknown and set up a business in an exotic location. In Bali, he has low business rates and labour costs to his advantage.

He is also sensible in augmenting his income with a job until he establishes himself and blessed with a supportive family who are helping him distribute from the UK.

But what impressed me most was his passion, positivity and creativity.

5

Asher Budwig

CEO Lola's Cupcakes

www.lolascupcakes.co.uk

I've known Asher's father, Mario, for many years and have always been impressed by his entrepreneurial approach, paralleled with his humanity. I've always seen how he's been quietly interested in charitable projects as well as his own development.

He's always struck me as having a similar outlook to mine yet always 'on' whereas I spend quite a bit of my time more sedately.

In my early business life, was I always busy too? I realised that I must have been.

For a while I was running two companies, Cable London and Broadsystem simultaneously, for example. But in the early days, it never felt like work because I enjoyed it so much.

Anyway, Mario suggested I interview his son Asher, who had the reputation as a Super Mario! Here he is…

I started my business career at about the age of 12. I had a keen interest in being a DJ, so I purchased some disco decks and my dad was my roadie.

I would put an article in the JC (Jewish Chronicle) and we would receive bookings and go out and do kids' birthday parties. I was really quite young at the time, but nonetheless prepared. I'd put a set list together and ran the events.

I remember charging about £150 and started renting out some of the equipment and that was my very first start as an entrepreneur, but from then school and studies took over.

Then as I approached my A levels, I started a jeans business called X Label Jeans. I was going to Primark, buying jeans at £4, bringing them home, dyeing them, ripping them up and putting a label on them, branding them X Label Jeans, and then through a network of friends, selling them.

Each salesperson was receiving commission on every sale they made.

And throughout my years as a kid, I had many books, where I'd always write down ideas. Lots of ideas. One idea I had was a restaurant that would have cuisine from all over the world and each area would be branded and designed for the cuisine that you were eating. You could hop from one to the other.

Some ideas were ridiculous, some were more sensible!

Then I went on a Gap Year at 18, after my A levels, with three friends. And one of the places we ended up in was Guatemala. We stayed with a family while we were volunteering building houses for those that didn't have one.

And on the kitchen table, the person I was staying with, was making these chocolate dip frozen bananas. And I remember just looking and thinking, 'Hmm'.

At that point it was just a mental note for me.

Then I merrily went off to university and I remember during my first year I started thinking what I could do to earn money?

It was that summer that I started a stall in Camden Market selling chocolate dipped fruits. Originally it was just strawberries on a stick drizzled in chocolate. I had some ideas to do Milkshakes, which were all the rage, but there were lots of logistical issues around selling milkshakes in a market and fruit with chocolate sounded like an easier idea. From there on I did the frozen banana - that was in 2009, I think.

I would set up in Camden Market every Saturday and Sunday morning at six o'clock and work until eight o'clock at night.

I'd come down from university every weekend to run the market stall and then travel back up to Nottingham Uni arriving about midnight on a Sunday night. Everyone would joke that the week was my weekend and the weekend was when I was really working and working hard because I was putting in 13 or 14 hour days.

My bedroom became my stockroom and I had a supply of chocolate and nuts and all sorts of things which I would order to arrive at my home during the week in the very early days.

It brought in great income and the stores would take between £500 and £600 a day. We were grossing around £2000 each weekend.

I had a small team of staff, lots of different people I met along the way, some amazing people. One of the individuals I employed I'm still currently in touch with and she does a lot of graphic and design work for us. She's an incredible illustrator. You meet people and you carry them all the way through and that's always beneficial.

I did Camden for quite some time then Greenwich Market as well. So, we'd have two stalls going and we also did lots of events in the summer as well. Some of the Cambridge balls and festivals and some smaller private events.

I remember as it came to the last year of university, certainly towards my last exam, I said to myself 'I've got this great business running and it paid for me to get through university'.

I felt rich while I was at university because every weekend I would come back with a good income and could then buy all the food that I wanted and all the vodka to drink at the parties. I really felt independent, which was really, really important to me.

Then when I'd got my degree in Management Studies, I said to myself, 'I'll give myself a year but you can't build your whole career on the Market because it's such a volatile place and you need to have strong foundations'.

I spoke with my father-in-law and he put me in touch with Vida E Caffe. I worked for them for a couple of months. They're the Starbucks of South Africa. I helped them run and operate three of their stores.

At that point my dad turned to me and said, 'Look, Lola's Cupcakes, started by two girls, is for sale. Would you be interested in working with me?'

And I remember him bringing home a box of cupcakes. And I looked at it and thought, 'Well, that's interesting'.

We started the Lola's venture nine years ago. Lola's had a reasonable turnover but wasn't making lots of money, but it had a really strong, following, strong brand and strong presence in the market. It was servicing three stores and doing some home deliveries.

It was really a bit of a hobby business, a bit of a craft business, but nonetheless an operating business.

And in the early years we just tried to professionalize it and organise things so there was a bit more order to it. And slowly, day by day, and month by month, the business grew and has grown significantly over the last couple of years.

Thankfully back in 2011 it was one of the earlier companies to have a good and working online presence so people could go order cupcakes and have them delivered.

Then we started opening more stores because we originally thought we'd go down the cafe route but we learnt later on that that might not have been best because cafes are very expensive and more challenging to operate than small mobile units.

Then we also experimented with Transport for London, opening small retail carts dotted around the Capital. They were very good for us because they had a relatively small level of capital expenditure, generating lots of income from the passers-by. All the hungry commuters, and those wanting gifts for special occasions.

Around 2015, we started to understand that online was going to be important and put our attention there.

We always focused on quality, customer service and occasions such as Halloween, Christmas, Valentine's day, and really pushing on those days to stand out.

Marketeers would say, give people a reason to buy and engage with the brand to shop.

From there on we've grown the number of stores from 10 to 15 to 20 to 25 with a portfolio of small carts, kiosks and shops and the focus on online.

More recently we launched some collection lockers. I think we were one of the first companies in the UK to launch a click and collect service for food that wasn't owned by the supermarkets. So that's been where a customer goes online, orders the product and picks up from one of our collection points. And one of the most ingenious things we did was put one of them in a Phone box.

That all came about because I was a market trader myself and I used to receive Market Traders Federation magazine.

And I remember seeing the Phone box in there and thinking 'What could one do with a Phone box to actually generate income from it'.

Then I came across this Click and Collect locker idea and I thought that would be interesting and we've now got almost 15 lockers across the Capital.

We also launched a postal brownie service back in 2018 which was basically looking at companies that have been very successful like Bloom and Wild who were doing letterbox flowers.

And it was just because we'd been selling a lot of brownies in our business and thought we could sell them through the post and reach a wider audience. We could never deliver to the whole of the UK because the cupcakes are too fragile to post and had to be hand-delivered by a van.

Brownies got around that problem. So, we launched brownies by post and have been very successful. And following that we launched various other products through the post, such as Create a Cake kits. We send the sponge and icing ready to go. You simply just create your cake.

That's an overview of the company. We employ about 400 people as of 2020.

One of the things that we've always done is try wherever possible to promote from within and grow people. Most of our senior management joined us in the early days. Of course, we've also pulled people from the outside who have been brilliant.

There's definitely a level of benefit to finding people that are experts in their field and bringing them in. But I think it's always been good for people in the company to know that some people started at the bottom and were given opportunities.

I had a warehouse chap who came from Romania. He was staying with his brother at the time and his family were in Romania and it's often quite sad to hear that families have been split up as part of their economic struggle.

Anyway, he started in a warehouse and then slowly let us know that he had some skills in photography, and he taught himself how to 3D render on a computer. He's now full time in our marketing team.

Then there's a chap who started as a shop assistant in our store in Westfield Shopping Centre. He's now a full-time videographer. Also, the Area Manager and the Operations Manager of our retail business started as team members.

So homegrown talent is significant in our business. That's one of our grounding principles.

Stephen: You highlight the fact that you go above and beyond the normal. You try and give back something to the staff.

Asher: Charity has always been important to me personally and also as a business. We are approached daily by charities and we allow the business to give back in an organized fashion.

Lots of people have asked if they can have cupcakes for bake sales or if they can pick up stock at the end of the night and donate it to causes. And we've always facilitated that on a case by case basis.

And a couple of years ago we decided to support the charity, Spread A Smile, who look after seriously ill children, and entertain them in hospitals.

We donate a vast amount of cakes and cupcakes that they send out to their network.

And at the moment we're selling antibacterial sanitiser on our website as one of our responses to Covid 19 and it's completely not-for-profit and all profits go to Spread a Smile.

We always donate a thousand cupcakes every month to charity.

And we do look after people. There are obviously lots of basic benefits that employees enjoy when they join the company. Some of them we don't shout about perhaps as much as we should. We have run English lessons for quite some time for all the team in the bakery and the wider business for those that need it.

And we've launched our grocery service to all our customers, and we prepare boxes of food for all our team every Monday that they can come and collect, and we also sell all our products at cost price to our teams.

We have performance-based pay systems. I think it's really important to align the goals of everyone in the business. And there's profit share schemes at store level, right from the team member all the way up to the manager.

It's important that everyone feels a sense of achievement for their hard work and all their efforts.

And if someone isn't able to come to work due perhaps to an accident we always try and help people wherever we can to make sure that they would be treated as we'd like to be treated. And I think that's kind of the mantra that we've taken through the business over the years.

We're a team, we look after each other, we respect each other, we understand the situations that some people find themselves in and we help each other. That's the flavour of the business.

As the business grows, it's very easy to write slogans on the wall. That may work for large companies. But I think what we have done is to select the right kind of people who embody and deliver upon the same values that we have in the way we want situations to be handled.

You can try and recruit the kind of people that you believe care in the same way that you care and would take the same decisions and write the email as you would write it. It's not going to be a hundred percent Bulletproof approach, but I think it's the strongest foot forward in trying to ensure that you've got the right people on your team and that your company acts in the way that it should. Both outward and inward.

Success for Lola's is about allowing its team to be successful in the future. We want to support our team and we want to never let our team down.

But we tell staff, '400 people depend on you doing this well and those 400 people support many more thousands of people whether it's back home or here'.

Putting that into perspective for someone can really often help when you're dealing with a tricky situation where we might not have taken the right action.

My roadmap is simply to grow the business, develop the business, make sure the business is doing good, make sure it's caring for the environment that it operates in.

We were one of the first companies in London to operate refrigerated electric vehicles. A good proportion of our fleet is already electric and refrigerated, which is amazing. And you know, the drivers appreciate and enjoy being part of that. They want to be part of a company that looks after the environment. So, I think the roadmap is to do good to the environment, do good to the people in the business, look after the customers properly and everything will be OK.

We are also health conscious. We try to help customers as much as our own teams. There are lots of people out there with dietary requirements that can't have gluten and can't have dairy. So, we've gone along that road at Lola's.

Personally, for me, providing I can look after my family, enjoy what I do and stay healthy, nothing else really matters.

Stephen: What I've noticed with entrepreneurs is that there comes a point when they might sell the business, or they may have made a ton of money that they weren't expecting. And some of them carry on doing business after business. Some of them go into charitable foundation work, some of them do a combination and some of them retire.

Asher: I hope I'm on the combination front.

I've got a thirst and energy for doing what I'm doing right now. We've been supportive of a lot of charities over the recent years, so I hope to be able to do both. You talk about selling the business, but I've learned that it may not often be the best thing to do. It's about appreciating and being happy with what you've got. A regular, stable income is perhaps on occasions better than a big pay cheque.

I think to find a good business and nurture it and create it and find all those right people takes such a long period of time. Would you really want to say goodbye to your enterprise because of receiving that pay cheque? Selling out of a business is a bit like saying goodbye to all your extended family, or it would be in my view.

Stephen: In the pandemic, you suddenly went into grocery business from scratch. That was brave?

Asher: It wasn't a very brave decision. When I started my career as Banana Man many years ago in Camden Market, I would often go to the fruit market and just have a little look around but I would have a company deliver me fruit because it was convenient, and I didn't want the extra hassle of buying my own fruit.

When Lola's decided to start groceries that was a very comfortable move because I knew a lot about the markets. I was already sending someone to the markets every evening buying fruit because we know that you get better quality products than relying on someone else to pick it and deliver it for you. So, I simply added new products and got them brought back to the bakery, photographed them, and put a few collections together in boxes.

I think that has been incredibly valuable for Lola's. We have an in-house photographic team, in-house marketing team, in-house videography team. Everything's in-house. We have an in-house e-commerce team, in-house SEO team, in-house accounts. And that allows us to react quickly and adapt.

We are actually turning over more money during the pandemic and that is due to the collective efforts of the team. The team has done an incredible job.

As for suggestions or recommendations or ideas for the young entrepreneurs, I'd say as you go along your journey, try to own as much of what you do as possible. I'm not saying you need to build your own call centre software to handle calls, but try to own the activities that you do and do as much as you can in-house because it will grant you the flexibility and freedom and speed in the future to react to situations that change.

But the first thing to do is actually just get out there and do something, whatever you might be interested in doing or think you want to do. Look into that, study that and research that and try and get yourself involved in that sphere or forum.

And if you're successful doing that, brilliant. But if you struggle or if you're struggling at the moment, this challenge in some way, shape or form will enhance and develop your thoughts and your own experiences.

And that will lead to things. I think things always lead to other things. So, the more you do, the more people you speak to, the more advice you seek, the more successful you're likely to be.

That would be my mantra. Do more, get out, talk to people and get yourself involved in something, even if it's not exactly what you want to do. But ultimately you have to follow your own intuitive thoughts.

I was very moved by my interview with Asher.

He was passionate throughout, but really became fired up when talking about his fellow team members.

This approach epitomises to me Authenticity in Business. Simply treating your organisation as a family complete with family values.

Another thing I liked was that Asher always tries to foresee future obstacles and plans for how he realistically could overcome them. Often people I meet think that simply by being positive everything will be OK. Positivity is important. But all too often I see too much optimism and not enough practical forethought.

Anybody could have foreseen the importance of online, but Asher embraced it.

Virtually nobody could have foreseen the pandemic but Asher's planning put him in a great position.

I'll be following his future enterprises with keen interest.

6

Jason Kirk

Founder, Kirk And Kirk

www.kirkandkirk.com

Jason is my first cousin and the only member of my generation to stay in the family optical business.

Getting the impulse to run an enterprise came suddenly and was a huge shock to me, but then I remembered that my grandfather and his brother were great entrepreneurs.

They were also tap dancers and were both charismatic but also eccentric.

Kirk Family 1927 – Grandpa Percy, Uncle Sid, their wives Sarah and Miriam, their children and friends

An unsubstantiated report is that they worked on the Argentinean Railway as Accountants for different departments but only one was qualified. The pretend Accountant used to look busy all day and then bring the books home for the real Accountant to complete!

However, it is a fact that in the UK they founded Kirk Brothers, which designed spectacle frames and had the patent for the little piece of movable plastic that some frames have at the point they sit on the nose. The name for these is 'The Facifit Nosepads'.

Somehow the next generation became convinced they HAD to enter the optical trade despite the fact that my grandparents had accidentally wandered into the trade and could have equally become professional tap dancers for at their height they appeared on a stage in East London with Harry Houdini – the great escapologist.

Nevertheless, virtually all their male heirs entered the optical trade and so I can only assume there was some pressure to do so despite the fact that the Kirk Brothers headquarters in Central London was bombed in the Second World War and was uninsured causing them to become well-off rather than wealthy.

My father became an optician but was also a funny man and wrote kids stories (never to be published and subsequently lost) and was a regular broadcaster on a London local radio programme called You Don't Have to be Jewish.

He also had an alter ego and had a yearly meeting in St. James Park with a mysterious Colonel.

Only years later did his brother Stanley tell me that Dad was a secret agent for the Israeli secret service at the end of the war and before the Partition of Palestine and the Colonel was his intermediary. Apparently, the Israeli Government wanted to give Dad an Honour, but he refused it.

Uncle Stanley himself established a lens making business in New York whilst also having a career as an extra on film sets. He had two business cards. One with a photo of him with a wig on and the other without so he could get double the work!

I asked Stanley's son Rob about Stanley's acting 'career':

"As you know, he was always quite a 'ham' and interested in performing. He did a little bit of acting in plays at the Synagogue but never really pursued it. But when I became a filmmaker, he was tremendously supportive of my career and I was able to give him parts in some of my productions. These roles earned him his SAG Card. (Screen Actors Guild).

So, when he retired and moved to Florida he decided to pursue acting more seriously. He created his resume that included the parts he did for me and those Synagogue performances turned into 'Off Broadway' roles. From that he got an agent and started to actually land some bit parts. The big claim-to-fame was Hume Cronyn's stand-in in Cocoon: The Return (Cocoon II). So, he was on set for the entire production and was included in the cast photo at the end of the shoot. From all this success, he eventually became President of the South Florida chapter of the Florida Motion Picture and Television Association".

I have to confess, that with an Uncle pretending to be an Accountant, a father who doubled as a Mossad agent and Uncle Stanley who invented his acting career, it does seem extraordinary that I should be writing a book on Authentic Business!

Anyway, it was my fate to be third generation associated with the family optical business and by then the 'rules' had been established and as far as my Dad was concerned the die had been cast and I was to enter the optical trade.

Looking back, I imagine his desire was to make Grandpa Percy proud of him with my help. Dad had been left with a small optical wholesale business following the bombing of the Kirk Brothers headquarters.

Once I had decided to take a different path, I imagine he was deeply disappointed and therefore sold that business to another optician with whom he formed a small chain of dispensing opticians.

Jason Kirk and I have been on parallel tracks. We're both entrepreneurs but Cousin Jason is the only one of my generation who has followed in the footsteps of his father.

He's also had his ups and downs but now seems to be on an upswing having established Kirk and Kirk with Karen, his wife.

By the way, I am a hopeless tap dancer!

Now let's learn from Jason…

My Dad had a small country practice. He was an optician in St. Giles and also had a practice in North London. And it was not very interesting to me at all. Esme and Neville, my Mum and Dad, were in the practice together. It was entrepreneurial in the sense that it was their own business and they went their own way.

But it felt very dry and conservative to me. What we do today is very different.

Karen, my wife and I design and distribute our own range of glasses called Kirk and Kirk, and we sell them all over the world to independent opticians. It's very design led.

It's unique in the products that we use and the way that the frames look and feel. It has a very distinct personality. It's almost a diametric opposite to what my Dad was doing.

When I was growing up, I didn't wear glasses until I was about 12 or 13 and I went through all the normal things that boys do when they have to wear their first pair of glasses. And it was a stigma that I didn't enjoy.

I didn't find a frame I liked, and I didn't associate my eyewear with anything fun or interesting. My Dad would remind me that my grandfather was in optics as well as his cousins and there was a whole family dynasty and none of my generation was in optics - but nothing could persuade me to go in that direction.

I went to university, studied French, then had a job in advertising and worked for a publishing house, selling advertising for about four or five years. And then I went to work for L'Oreal in sales and marketing.

One day, my Dad was clearing out his practice as he was going to decorate, and he asked me to give him a hand.

He said, 'If you like any old frames you can keep them'.

The Authentic Entrepreneur

Then I opened this one box and there were all these beautiful upswept green and blue glasses that it turns out my grandfather Sidney had designed.

I took a week off work and put sunglass lenses into those frames. Then I went up to London and banged on the door of all these clothing shops and said, 'I've got these great sunglasses and what do you think?'

Fortunately, they loved them.

I went back into L'Oreal on Monday and the very first day that I went back, they made me redundant. It was a complete coincidence!

I used the redundancy money to make some more glasses. That was 1992 and here we are in 2020 and we're still making designer frames and selling them all over the world to opticians. I think potentially it might compare to what Sidney and Percy were doing when they started up in 1919. They had a very entrepreneurial approach and were really trying to drive forward the optics industry.

Karen and I were trying to create something different. We would go and look at all the shops and see what they were selling and doing. And I can remember picking up the phone and speaking to an optician who was in Bordeaux and that was exotic. That felt hugely international. It was an interesting and challenging time.

We soon ran out of the original frames my grandfather had designed, but we would find caches of original materials from the fifties and sixties. They had just been left in some glass maker's shed, and we would buy those materials and then go and make new frames from old materials.

We built up a very distinct message and a very strong brand identity. We were doing okay, and my ambition was limited. I was a 25 or 26-year-old, just starting my own company. I was delighted that the company was surviving. I was happy to be able to pay my rent. We were driven, but it was a different kind of ambition.

As a youngster in that kind of position all the people around you just encourage and pat you on the back and tell you you're doing brilliantly.

We were very lucky. We had a great support system around us and then we'd been going for about three years selling to opticians and clothing stores. At that point we were only selling sunglasses and we were invited to be featured on The Clothes Show.

They did an eight-minute feature on us and everybody watched it! That eight minutes on prime BBC TV was amazing.

But we rang our clients and discovered that they weren't actually using our visibility to sell our products or buying more products from us. They were using us to attract people into their stores to sell other products that they had in stock. That was hugely frustrating because we were getting calls from consumers who wanted to know where to buy our products.

At that point we took a very risky decision to open our own store in Covent Garden. It was very different to any optician that anybody had ever seen before. And it had a very fashionable presentation. All the stars of the time, music and actors used to come in regularly and became our friends.

Stephen: How did that happen? Normally, if you open a shop, you don't expect it immediately to be attracting that sort of clientele.

Jason: I think it happened because the glasses were so different, and we had a different approach to optics. We were interested in the style aspect and the way the glasses made you feel. We didn't necessarily know how to articulate the things we've learned to articulate now. But it was very much about what your glasses presented about you and how you can present your personality. And we did it within the constraints of the technology of the day. Daniel, your son, designed our first website. We didn't even know what a website was!

It was word of mouth. We were not in the main streets of Covent Garden, but people enjoyed wearing our glasses as opposed to just being functional things. And I think that was always the difference.

We talk about user experience now, but it was a long time before anybody was talking about it, but that's what we were trying to create. We did personal styling and designing for the biggest bands of the day. And it's lovely because we've remained friends with a lot of those people as well.

Stephen: Then eventually you brought in outside investors to your first company Kirk Originals.

Jason: It was much later. We were satisfied with the growth that we had. The company was growing. We were turning over probably just under a million pounds by 2007, 2008. It was modest, but it was great.

We were very proud of what we had achieved. We realised that we had built a brand that people recognised and we found after 15 years of creating different eyewear, people knew our products immediately. If they saw someone walking down the street in Boise, Idaho, wearing a pair of bright blue glasses of a certain style, they knew they were Kirk Originals and that was very gratifying to us.

But there was so much more potential and the only way that we could fulfil that back then, was to take on some sort of investment to allow us to grow. We had no shortage of ideas, no shortage of great people around us. But what we didn't have was the finance to make those things happen.

So, we went out looking for investment and we found it way too easily. I think sometimes if your product or service is very visible especially when it's fashion related, it's not necessarily difficult to attract interest. We had some private individuals who liked the potential of what the company was and very quickly came along and invested.

But soon it became clear we didn't share the same vision as the investors. They invested for money. They didn't invest for the love of eyewear or for the love of Jason and Karen Kirk. And I think the potential that they saw in our company was a brand which was well established and visible. But they wanted us to make a more general product and they wanted to reduce our overheads. They also wanted to change the model of how we actually got to the public. And it conflicted with what Karen and I had always felt was the right route for the company.

In hindsight, I learnt that it can very, very easily go wrong because the interests and the desires of founders are not necessarily the same as those of external investors.

We started that company in 1992 but in 2012 Karen and I realised that there was no future for us. And we walked away with the agreement of the old company and not knowing what we were going to do next.

But a few months later we decided to take our experience and goodwill in the optical world and set up Kirk and Kirk which was focused on pursuing optics with our ideals. We wanted people to be excited about eyewear. We didn't just want to make the most money possible.

I've had the benefit of other people's experience and advice over the years. Before I set up our first company back in the nineties, my dad introduced me to the marketing director for Curry's electrical retailer. And I can remember his emphasizing that in every piece, in every communication we should tell the story about my grandfather and finding the glasses. And that stuck with me.

And the very first time that we went to a trade show in New York, I bumped into Barbara McReynolds, who was one of the owners of LA Eyeworks and I was in awe. I was wandering around New York and I was in this antique shop and she was standing there. She's somebody who's really established in our industry. So, I plucked up my courage, introduced myself and asked for one piece of advice.

She said, 'Stick to your principles'.

And that's nearly 30 years ago.

When we set up Kirk and Kirk, that advice was at the forefront of our minds. It was very important to make sure we could run the company viably of course, but also to be making products people would love. If you provide the right customer service, people will come back to your company and they will tell their friends.

This time before we even set up the company, we knew we needed outside investment. We knew how much it costs to design, research and produce a collection of glasses that you can sell, to go to a trade show, to set up reps, all of those things. We knew that it was going to be financially challenging and extremely risky.

We did the business plan, put everything together and went to investor forums.

I also went to an old friend who's a partner at one of the big finance firms in London and he looked at our plan and decided to invest. We then had great investment from a partner that we trusted. We could set up without having to look over our shoulders all the time.

Then we let the company grow for a couple of years, establishing ourselves and the proof of concept.

Then we went to raise money again because it was clear that to fulfil our potential, we would need more money.

There are Government schemes designed to help entrepreneurs attract money, especially in very young and early stage companies. Schemes like SEIS and EIS are very, very helpful when you're trying to attract investment.

The finance was very important, but even more so was having investors we could trust and that we felt had our interests at heart.

Eventually we found a company based in Milton Keynes called Growthdeck. They are a membership club of investors and they recommend investments to those investors. These days the investors are referred to as Angel Investors.

Growthdeck do all the research and due diligence before they propose something to their investors. They have been absolutely superb, and our interests are aligned.

They were also at great pains to point out that there is no value to a design-led company if you take the founders away or if the founders aren't motivated.

If we needed some expertise in a particular area and didn't necessarily know somebody, they would help us.

They protected their investment by having someone on our Board with our consent as a Non-Executive Director. They also recommended a Chairman, Hugh Clark, who is from the Clark shoes family.

He has been amazing to work with. The brilliant thing that he's done is ask us questions all the time. But never once has Hugh said you ought to do this. That is great leadership. Having a good Chairman, plus having a good Non-Executive Director, having somebody who is impartial but interested is really, really valuable.

Stephen: Looking ahead, what are your aspirations for the future? And if you were to give people starting in business some advice, what would that be?

Jason: The advice that goes through your whole career is listen to people and be aware of what you don't know. Try and find out what you don't know. That doesn't mean learn it. That means be aware of it so that you can find advice, find guidance from people who have more experience. There are very few people that know how to do everything. I haven't met any!

In terms of investment, there isn't one size fits all. For example, I looked at crowdfunding and it's brilliant. I've seen some people do really, really well and I also saw challenges with it in terms of the amount of time that it takes and the fact that you need to have a certain amount of investment ideally before you actually go on a crowdfunding mission.

So, look around, speak to lots of different people. It's very tempting when somebody says, 'I want to give you a certain amount of money', to think that's amazing. It's very flattering to anybody, but actually it's not necessarily the right thing at the right time.

I'm third generation in the optics industry. The previous two generations put so much into optics so that's driven and motivated me.

Right now, in the pandemic, I'm really concerned at how the independent sector of optics is going to shape up when we come out of this current situation. How it's going to look and how equipped everybody is in the industry to deal with it.

In terms of Kirk and Kirk our principles haven't changed. We're still going to make glasses that people will love wearing. It's about making you feel amazing when you wear your glasses. At some point there'll probably be an exit. But we love what we do now.

Before the pandemic started, the business was growing at an incredible pace. We'd been doubling every year with the help of investment because that's allowed us to pursue some of the projects that we wouldn't have been able to pursue otherwise. And I see no reason why we shouldn't get back onto that track fairly shortly. It'll be a different environment and we'll just have to adapt to that new environment.

I love waking up and going to work!

I always enjoy learning about Jason and his adventures. After all, we are first cousins and come from the same gene pool.

I was obviously intrigued to see how he managed to stay in the family business by being creative and using our grandparents' spectacle designs to launch his own company with Karen.

I was also struck by his bravery in walking away from his first business because the aspirations of his investors were at odds with his own ideals.

Then he used that challenge to begin anew, with investors who understood him better and were prepared to support his dreams.

Lastly, what a coincidence that he had just finished a book raising money for charity just as I started mine. Therefore, he was able to share with me his experience of the book publishing process. What were the chances?!

7

Monica Dodi

Serial Intrapreneur And Entrepreneur

I first met Monica in 1987, when she had just begun her term as an 'intrapreneur' at MTV. Believe it or not, MTV had only recently launched in the States, so it was essentially a start-up and Monica had been recruited for her entrepreneurial abilities to do deals with the embryonic UK cable industry, which had only just begun. It was also helpful that she bumped into the founders of MTV at a party.

As you'll remember, I entered the industry after resigning my final 'job' because I fell out with my boss over a fridge door. Such are the seemingly small events that guide a life.

UK cable TV was just beginning, and the UK Government was seeking bids from potential operators. Luckily, they were asking for 'interactive' expertise. This was far-sighted because back then nobody had heard of the internet. It was realised that cable could offer a return path for subscribers to feedback their responses directly to an operator.

Even luckier perhaps, I was already a Non-Executive Board member of Windsor Television – one of the very first new operators as well as working on an election polling programme for Granada TV, where voting projections were made for the first time using a telephone panel, who could vote in real-time throughout the TV programme.

The fact that I knew nothing much about business then didn't seem to matter and I had relatively no trouble recruiting a Board and investors and use of offices in Camden Town, which was rapidly becoming a media hub and the eventual London home of MTV.

My arrival in Camden was also providential. An early investor was a company called Research Recordings, run by Mike Abrahams and he and I had become friends.

One day, whilst looking for offices for Cable London, my cable start-up, I was rushing out of a meeting at Capital Radio excited that I had been invited by Mike to his media cocktail party. So excited in fact, that I walked straight into a lamp-post, nearly knocking myself out, and suffering from concussion. I debated with myself whether this was 'a sign' to go home but my strong intuition was to attend the party. I hailed a taxi, and rather dazed, I chatted to Mike who, hearing of my need for offices, offered me space. I became not only a client of MTV in Europe but also their neighbour.

Monica was having trouble signing up the cable providers because MTV wanted a nominal payment per household. At the time, we had only cabled 30 flats in Gloucester Avenue, Camden, whilst we raised additional funds to cable the whole Borough. Therefore, the outlay for us was minimal and I was happy to sign the first UK MTV contract.

The other operators were livid, but it seemed a fair deal to me. I couldn't see how, in those early days, MTV could make any money on a tiny subscriber base, nor why anybody would sign up for cable if there were no programming.

Monica and I soon became friends. We had a similar outlook on life and are in touch still after many decades.

Before going over to Monica, here's a picture of me pretending to dig up Gloucester Avenue, Camden to lay the first cable with Chairman Jerrold Nathan and Executive Assistant Jan Roddy admiring a piece of equipment!

Right now, I'm working as Executive Director of Lord of Trees Foundation, a drone tree planting start-up out of Australia with global ambitions.

They can plant 40,000 acres in two days with seed pods that respect the biodiversity so you have a family of trees that can coexist as nature intended. I'm very excited and there's definitely a for-profit side to it in working with mining companies, agriculture companies and governments, but also from a 'carbon-nomics' credit standpoint.

The CEO is an experienced Frenchman whom I met in France. It's interesting how life takes curves that you don't necessarily expect. I think part of being an entrepreneur is embracing opportunities as they arise.

I'm 64, so I'm excited to focus on something that I think surpasses anything else. Our planet is dying and so I really wanted to get involved in something that could address climate change.

The second thing I'm working on, which is kind of kooky, is that I own this craftsmen house which was built in 1910. It's the house I had before this house I'm living in and which has views all over Beachwood Canyon. I see the Griffith Observatory, the Hollywood sign. It's my dream home.

I've been renting out that craftsman house on AirBnB, but because of the pandemic, nobody wants it.

I got an offer from a developer to buy it at a very attractive price, but he intended to demolish it, so I'm in the process of moving it. I'm literally going to move the house and I'm looking for land right now.

They don't build that kind of house in California any more. It's the way our grandparents used to build houses to last forever and I love it. But it's too big. My kids have left home and that's why I decided to downsize to something that's prettier with the view.

But it would break my heart that somebody would demolish the craftsman house and it's a win-win situation because the developer doesn't have the demolition costs.

It will probably be about $100k plus the land which will probably cost about $50,000 a year to $100k, but then I could probably sell it for at least $1m. So, I'm making a profit out of saving something historic.

So those are my two latest projects.

I'm still involved with Women in Venture Capital. I've done that for 10 years. We launched it in 2010. I firmly believe that we need to invest in women entrepreneurs because the numbers have gotten worse. When I started The Women's VC fund with a Harvard business school colleague, a lot of our early investors were also from the school.

At that time Harvard was only 17% women and we were naturally a very close group and we knew there was a lack of capital going towards women entrepreneurs.

In 2010, 4% of venture capital went to female entrepreneurs. Now it's 2%. Sadly, it hasn't improved even though there are lots of funds popping up.

It's been great working with young, dynamic entrepreneurs. We've had a couple of very nice exits in a couple of our portfolio companies, but frankly, I am not a banker and that's essentially what you are as a venture capitalist.

You're not the one who's making things happen. And that's what I love to do. I like to be the one, not necessarily in charge, but at least part of a team that's creating something and making decisions and delivering results. That instead of writing cheques to the entrepreneurs, telling them what to do and then they end up doing whatever they want to do!

Stephen: How did you decide to get into business in the first place?

Monica: It probably started when I was a little girl. Both my parents came to America after World War 2 with nothing. My dad had been a Prisoner of War for a few years in Germany. He had been an Italian soldier and my mom was in Paris during the occupation. They met in Paris after my dad escaped and he was working at Renault as a dye maker. And my mother was working at Bank National de Paris and they met on a blind date.

They longed to start a new life. So, they came to America in 1950 and worked as domestics for wealthy people. Then my mom got her hairdresser licence. Fast forward, she became a hairdresser to the stars at Elizabeth Arden. She had Shirley MacLaine, Pat Nixon and Shirley Bassey as clients.

She was known for her scissors, her 'gamine' haircut.

My dad became a very well-known chef. He wrote a couple of books. He cooked for Kennedy, Frank Sinatra, Senator Javits, Senator Heinz. After school, I used to go and help him in the kitchen and be his sous chef, kitchen helper. He would make these lavish dinners because this was the sixties and the idea of gourmet food was almost non-existent.

Julia Child was just starting and that's basically how my dad learned to cook because he was watching her on TV!

In the early days, we didn't have a lot of money, but I think that helped me to learn how to be resourceful and not be afraid of hard work nor taking risks. I ended up being a very good student and went to Georgetown undergrad.

I have to say I did 16 years of Jesuit education and everybody's equal in the eyes of God and all that.

I was lucky. I thought anything was possible. I didn't even think about the fact that just because I'm a woman, I can't do whatever I want to do.

It's a continuation of war-time mentality because a lot of women had to step up during the war.

Then, I went to Georgetown on a full scholarship.

And when I graduated, I did not want to work in a corporation but didn't know what I wanted to do.

But I answered an advert for a marketing representative for a start-up in Rosslyn, Virginia, just across the river from Georgetown, and got the job.

This was 1977. There were only mainframe computers, no internet, fax machines were just starting. This company microfilmed engineering specifications because the only alternative was paper. And the founder was retired Colonel Hockett, a real gentleman.

He launched this company with Angel funding, and we sourced original copies of specifications and there were millions. We had specifications for nuclear submarines, canned asparagus, and we resold them like hotcakes, to all the military government contractors.

I was the first salesperson and I hired a bunch of retired military guys all over the country to sell our stuff and we ended up selling the company to a German conglomerate.

I had great mentoring from all those guys.

Anyway, I didn't know what to do after the company was sold, so I applied to Harvard Business School for a laugh and got in because I guess a lot of women weren't applying back then. That was an incredible experience. Not necessarily because of networking, but the brilliant minds from all walks of life.

In my class, we had a professional ballerina, a guy that was a Navy Seal and a fashion designer. So just having all different points of view was incredible and a lot of them are still friends of mine today - usually the more eccentric types!

After I graduated, I worked in consulting for Touche Ross, which was one of the Big Eight accounting firms at the time, just because nothing came across my path that really was enticing.

Then at a cocktail party on Long Island, I met the founders of MTV Music Television, and they told me that they were starting up in Europe and I said, 'Oh my God, I would love that job. I even have a French passport'.

So, a few weeks later I was on a plane to London. Yet again I think it's just jumping when the opportunity comes, and not being afraid.

Talk about taking risks! It was a greenfield as they say. We were dealing with over 16 countries, different rules. Even though there was the Treaty of Rome, every country had its own way of distributing cable channels.

It was complicated, but we ended up being the fastest-growing satellite channel in Europe and I met a lot of interesting people. It was again a start-up, so everybody had to do a little bit of everything.

For example, if Liz Nealon, who was executive producer happened to be in Munich, she would call on the Munich cable operator. If I happened to be in Zurich, I'd call on Claude Nobs who was the founder of the Montreux Jazz Festival.

I worked for MTV for about three and a half years. I hired people and ran advertising sales and research. It was just a lot of fun because we had a very diverse group of people and I think that's why we were able to accomplish so much. Just having different points of view from different walks of life.

But I fell in love with a Frenchman and decided to move to Paris. I was 33 and I really wanted to start a family, which I did.

I was recruited by a head-hunter to run the new division of Disney for licensed products. Up until that point, nobody really did any merchandising for movies. Now you see it all over the place, lunch boxes, t-shirts, posters.

The Little Mermaid doll made things take off. That was the era of Beauty and the Beast, The Lion King, the real heyday of Disney, and it was perfect for a young mother.

Our office was on the Champs-Élysées, and my boss was an African American, Dennis Hightower. Incredible, incredible guy. Brilliant. We were signing deals with different companies, big ones, small ones, but mostly big ones and consolidating our licensing business. It was a real cash cow. And that's when Hollywood realised, they'd been missing the boat on merchandising.

I saw the Disney licensees making so much money that I decided to start my own company. Michael Eisner, who was CEO of Disney at the time, wanted all the European divisions to move to Euro Disney and I was just not having that because my kids were still small, and it was a long commute.

So, I started a greeting card company with a Disney licence and recycled paper. We did deals with Boots Chemists, Monoprix and Carrefour. That was the beginning of putting the product together for retail establishments.

Then I got an offer I couldn't resist from American Greetings which was a big card company in the States and they wanted to have a European foothold for their international expansion plus the Disney licence and I sold out.

Looking back, I probably could have gotten a lot more for it, but my marriage was also not going so well, and I was fed up with the whole thing.

My mother was sick, and I think for both men and women when you are losing your parents, it's just tough especially when you have young children at home. It's not very easy on a marriage, to begin with. Even the best of marriages.

But then I got the sort of offer I was looking around for.

My husband and I had separated, and I was recruited by a friend to work at Warner Brothers.

I moved the kids, the dogs, the grandpa and ended up in Los Angeles. But that didn't last very long because as with most things, the only certain thing is change.

Time Warner bought Turner Television and then Turner wanted the programming from Warner Brothers.

Around that time AOL was starting and I was recruited to be their CEO for content.

I was an 'intrapreneur' – someone you can place a bet on to start a division within a company. And they wanted to create content for the internet. What's that?!! It was the dial-up days...

We recruited an incredible group of people from all walks of life: Techies, creative types, writers, young and old.

In less than a year we broke even, and we had three or four million people a day that were staying on for 20 or 30 minutes. I was really lucky about that. A lot of it is just timing.

But I left AOL after a few years because they moved everything to the East Coast yet again after another merger.

Then I worked at SoftBank Technology Ventures. They had raised a huge fund, $1.6 billion. It was the dotcom craze. That's when I saw that I was about the only woman in the room.

They supported me on the concept of the democratisation of the internet, so we created YouTube a few years before YouTube and it was called Oediv (video spelt backwards). People with webcams could post whatever they wanted.

It was an idea of one of my executive producers from AOL and I said, 'This is so cool'.

We had the technical team to do it and a couple of million dollars to get it going and then the dotcom bubble burst and we couldn't get our next round and we had to close shop. Then two years later, YouTube was bought out by Google for $1.6 billion!

Then we launched the Women's Venture Capital Fund with my friend from Harvard Business School, because I saw the sheer lack of capital invested by traditional venture capital companies in highly qualified female entrepreneurs.

I've also been involved with the LA River Revitalization project. I was a board member there for five years as well as a Foundation for the Frank Lloyd Wright Mansion which had been destroyed by the earthquake.

It's been a fun ride.

Being a parent, man or woman, can create this constant pull between their own work and their family. So, I always figured, I might as well be as successful as I possibly can, make as much money as I possibly can because that pull is not going to go away.

Stephen: In conclusion, what advice would you give to those considering being entrepreneurs?

Monica: I think you've got to figure out what's the worst that can happen because you can fail and it's okay to fail. I think a lot of people don't become entrepreneurs, not because they don't want to, but because they're afraid.

They're afraid that people are going to make fun of them. They're going to ridicule them, that they're going to fail, that they don't know where their next pay cheque is going to come from.

People take a normal job for security, but that doesn't exist anymore anyway. Look what's happening right now here in the United States where the corporations are getting all the bailouts and they're still laying off people.

I think being an entrepreneur is more secure because you can be your own boss.

And I think you should be a passionate person, period. There are a lot of things that interest me, you know, there's just not enough hours in the day and I wish I could live another thousand years because there's just so many things I want to do. I think a lot of it is just your outlook on life.

Monica's passion, dynamism and energy fly off the page. Her willingness to take risks, move continents at a moment's notice and grab opportunities as they present themselves is quite unusual.

She was willing to jump into new ventures as an intrapreneur as with MTV and AOL or become an entrepreneur as with her card business.

Talking to Monica always makes me think that anything is possible!

I wonder what she'll be doing next!

8

Tracy Gray

Founder, We Are Enough and The 22 Fund

www.the22fund.com

Apart from the many interests Monica Dodi mentioned in her interview, she is also a Partner in The 22 Fund with Tracy Gray and highly recommended Tracy for interview. Tracy is a force of nature as you'll see...

When I graduated from college, I wanted to be an astronaut. That was my goal. Then I found out that you had to be a certain height because astronauts in the past were pilots and they were men. And the space shuttle technology was from the fifties.

They thought everyone was going to be a man. A short man would be maybe five, seven and you have to have perfect eyesight. I do not have perfect eyesight and I'm five, three, so I couldn't be an astronaut, but I thought the next best thing would be to work on the Space program.

I didn't work directly for NASA, but through an aerospace company and I was a mission monitor and systems engineer.

When the shuttle wasn't flying, we were connecting all the NASA installations around the country using the DARPA net, which was pre-internet.

The communications were my 'day job' because when the shuttle was flying, we had to be up 24/7.

Then I would monitor the missions and translate what the astronauts said to the Defence Department Generals at the Los Angeles Air Force Station (now the Los Angeles Air Force Base), where I was working.

My role was the mission monitor. I would listen to the Capcom (Capsule Communications) and was the only person who could talk to the astronauts, take notes, and then do a presentation to the Generals.

But then I was investigated by the Department of Defence and the FBI for being a subversive!

I was a progressive, a liberal and the Government at the time (and now!) thought if you don't agree exactly with the Government, you can't work for the Government.

It was my first job and I had all these posters that were very lefty in my office that was behind steel doors with a security code to get in. I was young and I thought 'screw you, I'm going to do whatever I want!'

They found that I wasn't a subversive of course, but I felt if I couldn't be myself and work in an industry I love, I wasn't going to stay there. But I stayed in engineering until around the late nineties and then I fell in love with the music industry.

A friend of mine is one of the top world-wide music managers. I'd go to these concerts and backstage, meeting all these performers. I thought 'That's what you do for your job? I want to do that!' Of course, that was one tiny piece of his job. The job itself was really hard.

Anyway, I was working for another music manager/record label friend who had a frat brother from Stanford, who was a venture capitalist in Silicon Valley but wanted to open in Los Angeles. There were only a handful of VC firms in Los Angeles back then.

So, he said to my friend, 'Why don't you come in and run this firm for me?' That's that network effect.

My friend had never been in venture capital before. And even though I was in the tech world, I had never heard of venture capital or entrepreneurship or startups. I didn't have that language, but I was asking him what he was doing and what he was investing in without really having the terms that we all know now like 'What are these business models? How do you make money?'

I was pretty much criticizing his investments. And he said, 'Well, instead of criticizing me from afar, why don't you come in and work for us and be our Analyst?' So that's how I got into venture capital.

Little did I know that it was so hard to get into venture capital because I just fell into it. Which is kind of my life, falling into things.

But I loved venture capital. I mean, one reason I was a music manager was because I don't like working on one thing. I like the diversity. I had more than one band of different types of music, so I couldn't get bored.

Being bored is like death to me. That is the driving thing for me all the time. And in venture capital and private equity, there's no way to be bored. You're helping companies do all different things, but you're not working in one company. But what I didn't love was who we were investing in.

As the analyst, I had all the business plans first, and the initial meetings, and I just saw a bunch of white men coming in and pitching for the money. We were giving $2 million away to two guys with ideas. And they were always white guys.

And it just didn't make sense to me at all. I'm an engineer, logical. One plus one equals two, evidence-based. And we were talking about companies investing in growing markets. Yet we were investing in a shrinking market of white men and it made no sense to me.

So, I left that firm thinking I could start my own venture fund.

But you cannot start your own venture fund after being just an analyst. Right? There's no way, but I thought I could!

I was very interested in the nexus between private capital and economic development and how it could be leveraged to impact different communities that weren't receiving this capital.

I felt women and people of colour were being left out of this whole equation. What could I do to bring the two together? So, to understand economic development, I went to work for an economic development nonprofit.

But I didn't like working within a nonprofit because I've been taught to make money. The whole thing around not-for-profit was just not for me. I'm not saying it shouldn't exist. It definitely should exist. But for me, it didn't work out so well. But I did learn a lot about economic development.

I also felt I needed to get my MBA for credibility.

A lot of women and people of colour think we have to line up all these degrees just to validate ourselves. I have to do so much more than your average white male has to do to become credible. So not only did I get my MBA, I got two MBAs from two of the top 10 schools in the world. I went to Berkeley and Columbia. They had a joint program, but you get degrees from both of them at the same time. Berkeley was more about social impact and entrepreneurial and Columbia was more Wall Street and finance.

I came out of the MBA programs and I was going to start my own venture fund investing in women and people of colour. Early-stage tech, which quite a few people are doing now, but no one was doing it then. We are talking around the beginning of 2008 and I was going to raise capital from people who supposedly cared about this issue. But they would say right to my face, 'Are there women and people of colour in tech?' Now I'm a woman, a person of colour and an engineer! But I'm sitting right in front of them and they're asking me if I existed! And I didn't know how to answer it. I was like, where ARE you? Do you not see me here? But that was the bias during the recession that continues today.

I got a seed investor in August 2008 and then in September 2008, it all fell apart. The recession started and there was no way I was going to raise any capital. I was looking for my recession gig and I became a consultant to the Los Angeles Mayor who needed someone to help them raise capital for affordable housing. And I came up with a strategy and raised around $35 million in six months.

Then I was done as a Special Advisor to the Mayor. So, they asked me to come in full-time because they were bringing in a billionaire to work for a dollar to be the Jobs Czar.

And the billionaire said to them, 'No one understands what I'm talking about. Not only do they not know what I'm talking about, but they also don't know that they don't know what I'm talking about'.

The Mayor thought I could translate because I understood what was happening in City Hall as I had been a consultant there and that I understood capital markets and investing. I had known The Mayor for 25 years at that point, but I wasn't interested in a political career. I wasn't interested in a career in a political office, and the whole power struggles that are there are not for me.

I was very interested in working for the billionaire because everyone needs a billionaire as a friend, right? So, I was like, okay, I will work for him. He left after a year to run for Mayor. And then I was going to leave because I don't like to work anywhere where I can't learn from either the person I'm working for or from the environment. There was nothing I was going to learn from anyone in that building.

Another friend became Chief of Staff and she asked me to stay. And I said, 'I will stay if I only report to the Mayor and I sit next to the Mayor and you, and I become a Senior Advisor for International Business'. She agreed and I stayed.

This is what led me to The 22 Fund in that during the recession under the Obama administration, the number one Economic Development and job creation tool was exporting.

Unlike most of the countries that made it through the recession, such as Brazil, France, Germany, Russia at the time, India - in The United States, only 1% of all our companies, small, medium, large exported. Whereas in Germany, 42% of the economy is based on exports.

We were a consumer-based economy, which is why we were hit so hard because we were based on people buying things.

People didn't have any money to buy anything. Because our country and our companies were so insular and didn't sell abroad, we had no one to sell anything to. So, we were hit really hard.

Increasing exports was the Obama Administration's Number One economic development and job creation tool.

Also, companies that export are more successful. And again, it's not rocket science, it's business 101 - diversify in multiple markets.

Then I saw that also they create jobs faster than companies that don't export. They're more resilient and have higher revenue. And the majority of business owners who did export were people of colour because a lot of these entrepreneurs have relationships or family or some connection to another country. They're not afraid of the other and they're familiar with the market.

The Number One reason why people won't export is they are afraid of being taken advantage of, not knowing the language, not knowing the laws, just a bunch of fear.

The Brookings Institute took Obama's initiative, the National Export Initiative and created the Metropolitan Export Initiative. They saw that cities were the way to really execute this. They chose Los Angeles as the first city to execute on this Initiative because of our location. We are the Gateway to the South and Asia. I led that initiative with the Brookings Institute to try to get companies to export. And while we were doing that, we saw that the ecosystem for exporting was fragmented and we did our best to bring it together. But even when you fix the value chain of exports, there was hardly any capital for these companies in the United States.

The only two places you could get export funding was from EX-IM Bank and the SBA - Small Business Administration. EX-IM is a quasi-governmental bank that provided capital, but there were so many regulations around it for small and medium-sized businesses, that it was difficult to get any money. SBA gave some capital, but with the regulations, it also took a long time.

I bring this up because if you look at the rest of the world, they support companies exporting by giving them capital.

There's so much support and that's why those countries do better. Right? We don't have that, even though politically Republicans and Democrats like it, we just still don't have it.

I went to private equity firms and venture capital firms I knew and said, 'Why don't you guys invest in these companies? They're more successful. It's less risky. They're more resilient and it de-risks everything. What every investor wants is to de-risk, Right?'

But because we weren't an externally facing country, our companies and our investors were just focused on this market in the United States. So, I was like, okay, then I'll do it. I'll start a fund that invests in companies to increase their export capacity.

Naturally, my passion is social impact. So, this one strategy of investing in exports without me having to do anything else clicks off other impacts that I want to make. The majority of the entrepreneurs in companies that export are people of colour and the manufacturing sector is our focus.

These companies are in Low- and Moderate-Income communities (LMI) because the land is cheaper. So, jobs and economic development will go to those communities. And they create jobs faster. Also, these are quality jobs. They are more likely to have healthcare and they are paying on average over $90,000 a year. These are quality, sustainable, clean jobs that we're trying to create. So that's The 22 Fund and that's why I started it.

It was originally called The 44 after the first 44 men, women and children of colour who founded Los Angeles. They were called, in Spanish, Los pobladores del pueblo de Los Ángeles.

I have friends who are Chinese and for them, the number four is symbolic of death, so not a good idea, and I'm like, 'Why didn't you tell me before I already named it?'

I looked back online and it turned out there were 22 adults of colour who founded Los Angeles. And therefore, you have

The 22 because we are in Los Angeles. So that's how I started The 22 Fund.

We started in early 2018 and we're raising $100m. It is really hard to be two women and two people of colour raising a fund - really hard. But we have a pipeline of companies that we can invest in immediately.

We're hoping to have our first close by the end of this year. It usually takes three to five years for people of colour to raise a fund now. It took white guys two years, but for women and people of colour it takes a lot longer and that's the systemic bias that exists in the financial system. You're hearing more about it now, but it's been around forever.

Even though we have de-risked it for investors, they still will find problems and the goalposts constantly move. One investor said no, and I didn't even know what the reason was. I couldn't figure it out. So, raising capital is very difficult.

The people who are investing in us tend to be women. People hear me speak and then they approach me.

Impact investors are our target, but it's hard to get them to move because they're so conservative. And when you're a first-time fund, it makes them nervous.

Monica Dodi is one of our partners and you know she has a stellar background. My other partner Rajan Kasetty has been in international manufacturing his entire life. But if we were three white men with the same background experience, no problem. So, it's been challenging. I won't lie. But we hope by 2021 we'll start investing because we have companies to invest in.

Stephen: Now let's talk about your other initiative, We Are Enough.

Tracy: We Are Enough came about when I was asked to do a TEDx talk and while I was preparing, I thought I was going to speak about being the only African American in about everything I did.

Then I started reading the research around women and I saw a couple of things. First, I saw that we control most of the consumer discretionary spending around the world. So, in your household, think about who decides what is bought. Most of the time women make the decision and then the men decide where the money is invested.

Research has shown that women are slightly better investors than men.

I saw that and then I saw that there were a lot of people trying to get more women to become entrepreneurs and more women becoming professional investors. No-one was talking to that everyday woman who controls most of the money in their households. I also saw that with women 85 to 90% of our capital goes back into our families and the community whereas with men it's 35%.

Additionally, women-led or owned business are more successful at every measure of performance but receive less than 2.8% of venture capital and only 6 – 8% of all VCs are women – for women of colour it's less than 1%, for Latino women it's less than .1% and for Black women, it's .0006%, a rounding error, even though Black women are the most educated demographic in the U.S. These numbers are down from 20 years ago when I entered venture capital. The numbers were 3% and 10% respectively. It's statistically impossible to go down like that organically. This is bias, pure and simple, especially since women are creating businesses and wanting to enter venture capital in greater numbers.

I saw those numbers, and then I saw that women don't invest. Now I've spent most of my career, begging, cajoling, shaming, and making white men feel guilty and do the right thing and invest in women or people of colour. But I don't have to do that if I get women to invest in women, one plus one equals two!

The UN has 17 sustainable development goals and they said that increasing women's wealth impacts most of these.

So literally the path to changing and improving the world is through women and increasing their wealth and we do that by educating women. The poorest of the poor at the 'base of the pyramid' to the heights of Wall Street.

All we do is educate them why and how to invest in women-owned or gender lens[1] businesses. During the recession, if women had the same access to capital as men, we would have come out of the recession years faster and created six to eight million jobs. If we just had access, equality.

All these nonprofits do similar things and I feel if you are doing the same thing, let's do it together. No one is doing what We Are Enough is by speaking to ALL women

We say, whether you have 25 cents, $25 or $25 million, whether you have a piggy bank or own a bank, you can take your capital, invest in women and change the world.

COVID has extended things, but in first quarter 2021, we'll launch a global campaign to get 3 million women to invest over three years into women-owned businesses or with a gender lens on the public markets. If we're successful, we can move $3 billion to women.

We haven't seen that happen before and we literally want to put ourselves out of business. I don't want to have a non-profit for the rest of my life. We want it to be so successful that women say, 'You don't need to tell us, we got this. We know how to do this. We're investing in each other. Done, we don't need you'. That's our goal.

Stephen: The majority of people reading the book will probably be based in the United Kingdom. Is there any way that readers can help your general cause?

Tracy: There's a network of women around the world who we want to tap into. I went to London with my co-founder Delilah Panio, who's the vice president of the Toronto Stock

1   Gender lens investing is the practice of investing for financial return while also considering the benefits to women, both through improving economic opportunities and social well-being for girls and women. The term was coined around 2009 and became an increasingly popular practice in the mid-2010s.

The Authentic Entrepreneur

Exchange. Then there's an organisation there called Gender-Smart founded by Suzanne Biegel. Then there's another organisation called SheEO that started in Canada then Australia, United States, New Zealand and this year they launched in the UK.

Stephen: Lastly, what advice can you give young entrepreneurs, especially to people of colour and also from LMI backgrounds?

Tracy: Well, I think for most women, women of colour and people of colour, we're afraid to fail because we don't usually get a second chance, right? Whereas if you look at the kind of ethos in Silicon Valley, the men there wear failure as a badge of honour that they failed at one startup. Then that gives them the experience to start another one.

I want women and people of colour to not be afraid to fail, to take the risks. I think of it as a mindset shift. I think of failure as practice; that's the only way you learn. No one came out of the womb perfect. I'm constantly learning and I'm constantly trying not to repeat the same mistakes I made before.

I like Einstein's quote, 'Insanity is doing the same thing over and over and expecting different results'.

Don't be afraid to fail, just see it as a learning moment and take more risks. We haven't been given all the opportunities that others have so we conserve everything, we protect everything, but we need to have broader thinking and take a little more risk and keep learning.

I'm a Buddhist so the foundation of everything I do is compassion and mindfulness. And I think also entrepreneurs should be more compassionate with themselves and compassionate with others and put ourselves in other people's shoes. We always have the wrong perception, creating the wrong story about someone who offended us or someone that's done something wrong, but we learn if we put ourselves in other people's shoes.

I meant to say that at the very beginning!

Well, as you can see Tracy is incredibly inspiring. She not only worked in rocket science; she is a veritable rocket herself.

When Tracy pointed out that many exporters have relationships or family or some connection to another country, I thought of Aron who has both a support network in the UK and Bali, having married a Balinese woman.

And of course, I was shocked to learn of the bias against women of colour. This and related issues have hit the headlines recently and I do hope Tracy is successful in helping to change the world for the better.

And on a lighter note, I was reminded of the only time I had the opportunity to go backstage. I was travelling to New York for a meeting and chatting to the girl sitting next to me, who turned out to be a friend of David Bowie. She was going to meet him backstage after his concert at The Beacon Theatre and asked me if I'd like to join her and attend the After Party. But it was late, I was tired and I had a meeting the next morning. So, I declined. Just saying...

9

Bernard Frei

Founder, Vintage Sports and World Rugby Shop
www.VintageSports.com wwwWorldRugbyShop.com

I met Bernard shortly after founding Broadsystem. He was first a competitor, then colleague and finally a friend.

The amazing fact is that sport and sports memorabilia are his passion, whereas I have zero interest in sport, especially team sports.

I was once invited as a VIP Guest of the BBC, who were a client, to a major UK Golf Tournament they were televising.

As a courtesy, I drove to the event, made small talk as one does, and then as soon as the match began (does anything actually happen in golf?), I slid out and began my drive back to my London office.

However, I couldn't find my way out of the golf course, because every path seemed blocked.

But I persevered and eventually found some grass I could escape over to the exit.

Upon arrival back at the office, I was greeted by a round of applause. Apparently, I was televised driving over the golf course with a police car following in hot pursuit. Well, the police car must have given up because I never did hear further!

Bernard also mentions my obsession with coincidences and relates one of his and this therefore seems an ideal moment to explain my views because my belief is that if you follow your unique path your life will be full of coincidences.

I once went to San Francisco where I knew one friend. I had no idea where he worked or lived.

I arose early and went for a walk from my hotel. And as I passed the nearest subway station, my friend walked out. What were the chances?

Well pretty small, but instead in marvelling in the experience we tend to minimise it.

I used to be just as guilty as anyone on this minimisation.

I was once in an elevator and somebody was saying, 'I know one person in Romania and the population of Romania is 20 million and I bumped into them by coincidence. What were the chances?'

I couldn't resist remarking that the chances were one in 20 million. The person scowled at me and I suppressed a wry smile.

Of course, that explanation diminished their experience. I hope they can forgive my remark! But the fact is that a one in a 20 million chance is an incredibly small chance.

But let's see what Bernard has to say…

I'm an online sports retailer. I run two businesses both based in Birmingham, Alabama.

VintageSports.com was launched in 2018. It is a passion that became a business. We sell vintage sports clothing, equipment, and signed memorabilia for football, baseball, soccer, rugby, hockey, cricket and many other sports. Our collection covers most of the major American and global sports and we have discovered and brought in rare and unique items like a framed Ice Axe signed by Sir Edmund Hillary, the first man to climb Mount Everest.

My second business is WorldRugbyShop.com, a business that I started in 1998. We are the leading online rugby retailer and wholesaler in the United States.

My mother is French and my father was Swiss. They emigrated to the UK in the 1950s. I was born in Brixton, South London in the sixties. My father was raised in a Catholic boy's orphanage in Switzerland. He had a strict Catholic upbringing. Prior to moving to London, he had been to the UK to check things out and he had been introduced to the London School of Economic Science.

(https://www.schoolofphilosophy.org).

There are some aspects of their thought process that ran along the lines of Buddhism and as a young family, we were all heavily encouraged to get involved.

Otherwise our father ensured that every spare minute of our time was taken up at whatever church function he could find. There was a period where I would go to Sunday School, Mass, Baptist Bible Study, Methodist community meeting, Boy Scouts and Mass again in a week. Later in life he confessed that he thought it was a good way to keep me out of trouble, but it certainly didn't help my footballing skills!

If the Jehovah's Witnesses knocked on our door, they were always invited in. I was taken to their gatherings on several occasions. So, I guess you could say he was and we became very aware of spiritualism.

Today I am not actively involved in any religion but I have significant interest in and respect people of faith. Alabama is a god-fearing part of the country and I believe my Father's enthusiasm for organized religion and spiritualism helped prepare me for life here.

I went to a sporting school. I have always been a sports enthusiast and tried every sport our school offered. There were many. I ended up focusing on rugby essentially because I could.

A few months after my 15th birthday I had a motorbike accident and spent the better part of 18 months recovering. I was stuck in a hospital in the South of France which improved my French, but little else. By the time I was walking again I had given up any hope of ever making it into further education. The school tried hard, but sadly I lost interest and took a job instead.

My first job was as a cost accountant's clerk under one of Margaret Thatcher's Youth Training Schemes. It gave me a great look into professional life.

I met my wife, Maye, in Paris. We lived together in Paris then Australia and now Alabama. We have two children and I'm very much at home here in Birmingham.

Stephen: What, if anything has your education of various religions done to your view of business?

Bernard: I have never reflected on this question before. Growing up in London, despite going to a catholic school, and having been forced to get involved in so many religions, I never felt it should have a label. I was never aware of any of my friend's religions. Some of us went to the same church but there was no badge. Looking back, South London was and still is full of people from all over the world and of every religion.

When I first got to Alabama, I had prepared myself for the 'what do you do?' question which, as you know, a British person would find difficult to ask.

Americans are very direct, and I quickly got used to it and found it a very useful question myself. But every now and again people will ask you 'which church do you belong to?'

About 16 years ago I partnered with a local Christian University called Samford in Birmingham. It's a fantastic local College. Over the past 16 years we have been lucky enough to host 111 interns from their business and sports marketing school.

Over the years I have noticed what a great job the school does of identifying bright young people. It's not a strict school but they have general rules of life that the students buy into, both during school and in their professional lives.

I can see how religion guides them for the good. I think if I had not had my own childhood exposure to religion, I would have found it far harder to grasp the value of their upbringing. I might even have been slightly wary of it. They tend to have a very straightforward, honest approach to life and therefore to work. And I seem to respond well to that. It's refreshing in terms of my professional relationships.

Separately the London School of Economic Science would have had an impact. There were a series of exercises that we undertook daily, 7 days a week. I hated them! Even the most basic chores became significant events. We would spend ages preparing in just the right way, thinking the task through, planning, checking the plan and then ever so specifically, executing. No task was started without a short pause and some meditation. This desire to find perfection felt mad back then but occasionally now it will help me get through a difficult project. It taught me to be relentless and this seems to have been a theme in several of my businesses.

Stephen: Can we talk about coincidence or 'signs?' Have you had any that have guided you?

Bernard: You helped me to accept coincidence. Because of your influence I actively seek them out. Coincidence offers new opportunities and I remain open to it, always. I love it when it happens.

I was in a cab once, had not spoken to you in a year and saw you from the window on a packed 6th Avenue in NY.

But one coincidence particularly sticks out.

My wife and I bought our first house in Birmingham in 1997 quickly followed by our first dog. I would walk the dog around our neighbourhood in the evening. He became friendly with another dog and then I became friends with that dog's owner, Alicia.

I ran a rugby newspaper at the time called RugbyRugby.com. The advertising model had not worked and so I shifted to e-commerce.

As a player I had trouble finding the right rugby gear in the US. My plan was to use my contacts in the world of rugby, to help me source and import rugby gear into the United States. At this stage Amazon was just getting started and the brands weren't comfortable selling online. There was a lot of resistance to e-commerce generally. The sports brands were slow to grasp the online opportunities and were wary of non-traditional retailers like me.

The largest rugby manufacturer at the time was based in New Zealand. They had refused to open an account with me. I persisted and finally bluffed my way into a meeting with their CEO in New Zealand.

I flew down full of hope and got there on time for my meeting. The receptionist looked mortified to have to tell me that the CEO had left that morning for the UK and that he would not be back for ten days. I was politely furious and after a few hours of back and forth I flew home, dejected.

Back in Alabama, I was retelling all this to my dog-walking friend Alicia. She was appropriately horrified that I had been asked to fly 8000 miles for a meeting that had been forgotten or judged unimportant.

Ten minutes into our moaning fest she stopped mid-sentence and asked me to repeat the name of the company I had visited, I repeated the name and she casually said, 'I think my friend just bought that company'.

Now there was no way that this could be right. Zero chance. I told her she was wrong, that there was no chance that her friend from California had bought a rugby company. She insisted, I remained sceptical. She called her friend, Hap, and passed the telephone over to me. Hap Klopp was one of the founders of The North Face. He confirmed he'd bought the business and that I should consider my account opened. We quickly became his largest customer in the United States.

Stephen: What an amazing story.

Moving on, one of the most difficult things I've found in business is to treat my competitors in an authentic way. Treat them the same way as I would treat my family or friends. How do you deal with them?

Bernard: I think you've always had a very open mind and I think your description of how you behave is exactly how you behave. I have learned a lot from your approach. You and I were competitors once and yet you welcomed me into several partnerships that became important to me.

Nobody teaches you to be competitive. Playing sports obviously shapes you. Growing up with four siblings certainly does but as I spent more time around professional athletes, I saw that I had to work hard in order to reach their level of competitive intensity.

Inspired by what I saw I set about trying to emulate that approach. I appreciated that in order to maintain friendships at work I would have to tone myself down, but it drove me and the feedback I received over the years seemed to indicate that I was over-aggressive. I am sure we all are at times.

Unlike you, I did not embrace competitors. I saw them as an enemy rather than an opportunity for growth. My goal was to be rid of them. I wasted a lot of energy, for all the wrong reasons.

Today I have learned that partnerships are a lot more fun. I try to find a way to build the right relationships with as many people as I can. I am much happier working that way and it makes us a better company. I try hard not to follow competitors if possible. I try to convince my teams to focus on making our business stronger rather than what the competition is doing but in reality, I am rarely afraid to adopt ideas that I have spotted elsewhere if they are better than ours.

Stephen: Now, a cynic might say, that's all very well. But what happens when you have a competitor who's absolutely determined to put you out of business? How do you feel about that?

Bernard: The way I deal with it is to make my business better; to focus on what I can control.

I'm certainly motivated by what I see better companies doing. I am open to ideas and to change, especially where I see things can be improved. But I no longer spend any energy trying to take competitors out of the marketplace. That is not always easy when someone is taking business away from you. But targeting a specific business, trying to outdo them, I don't think that is a positive thing. I get more traction focusing on what we do and trying to do it better. I've tried both approaches and I think you will live longer with this approach!

Stephen: Finally, can you give a couple of pieces of advice for someone who, for whatever reason, is moving into business for the first time.

Bernard: I share the advice I was given as a young man. If you have an idea just get on with it. Don't wait. Try it now.

More generally, I have always had amazing business partners. Each has changed my life in some way for the better. I recommend sharing your journey with good people if you can.

I was embarrassed by Bernard's compliments and almost deleted them, but I realised that we should never underestimate the effect we have on others. In this case my views on coincidence left a deep impression as did Bernard's coincidence with the supplier and seeing me walk up 6th Avenue.

Bernard's view on competitors was also enlightening, as well as the way it has developed over the years.

Lastly, he sheds a positive light on religion to offset my own rather sceptical view!

10

Sam Sutton

Founder, New Forest Activities

www.newforestactivities.co.uk

I self-published a book just after the 2008 financial crash entitled Enlightened Business. I expected the world of business to change dramatically but it didn't. Nor was my book a best-seller!

But I did receive a small but steady stream of compliments from readers including one from Sam Sutton who was running a business called Liquid Logistics.

Sam invited Luiza and me down to meet him in The New Forest. Not surprisingly his business focused on water sports and he suggested we go kayaking.

Well I have had a fear of water from a young age. In fact, fear probably would not do it justice. More like blind panic.

Strangely it wasn't always that way. At about age 8, I was the first pupil at school chosen to swim a width and receive a coveted Green Badge.

I proudly swam off but at the far side of the pool I was under water and didn't know how to surface. I thrust my hands up and down and completely lost the plot because there seemed to be no way to surface again and in desperation the swimming teacher, Mr. Herbert, had to jump in and rescue me – much to our mutual embarrassment!

Well from that day, I wouldn't go near water if you paid me and I did my best to avoid future swimming lessons with a variety of excuses.

At the end of the year, we had actually had a Physical Education exam which included a mark for swimming. I have to admit that it was with some sense of achievement that I received a final mark of 7% overall!

Anyway, this sudden fear thing continued to puzzle me.

Then during my active business years, I had an office in Sydney, which I would visit every 6 months.

The Managing Director there, Aileen Berry, was very competent and so my trip was really to show support for her.

And on one trip, Australian Bruce Gyngell, who had been CEO of TV-AM, had returned to Sydney to live and invited me to walk with him along the coast at Bondi Bay early one morning.

In 1956, Bruce had also been the first man to appear on Australian TV and was somewhat of a celebrity such that every few metres someone would stop him and say hello – many of whom he actually knew by name.

At the end of our walk, Bruce took me to the Rose Bay Surf Club, which is the oldest such club in Sydney and on an impulse, he asked Reception to produce an old logbook.

It was a record of all the members who had drowned surfing since the club had been founded around 1830 and as I looked down the list I came upon one name that sent shivers down by spine and I felt overwhelming panic, as if…well as if it had been me drowning for a split second.

I've always liked to believe in past lives and had a 'past life regression' some years ago. Then under light hypnosis, I found myself saying I was a ballerina called Gloria during the War! This revelation, given my clumsiness, rather eroded my faith.

Coming back to Sam, I plucked up my courage and Luiza and I did indeed go kayaking with him and once my anxiety had somewhat subsided, I actually enjoyed the experience. There is hope for me yet!

Here's what Sam has to say…

I'm the owner of New Forest Activities, an outdoor activity provider. Our experiences include canoeing, kayaking, a ropes course, and Laser Tag, which we adapt to our clients' needs.

Our clients could be mums looking for a birthday party idea, a family looking to escape modern life or business teams learning a bit about themselves as well as having some fun.

I set this particular business up in 2010, but before that, in 2003, I started Liquid Logistics. I was and still am passionate about Paddlesports, particularly whitewater kayaking. If the New Forest were blessed with mountains and rivers, I'd be out a lot more than I am nowadays.

To quench my passion Liquid Logistics was born and I wanted to get other people involved in the sport.

The New Forest had a resource that was not being used, in the Beaulieu River. We couldn't take people whitewater kayaking then because we were not qualified, but we could take them on the river.

And on my degree course, I met a great friend Richard, and we set up this Paddlesports business, which evolved over time into New Forest Activities and we started work with youth projects and business teams.

We also set up an Archery range and in addition we facilitated problem-solving team challenges.

We used to rent other activity centres for some of the residential elements of our Prince's Trust programmes. And it seemed natural and organic to grow the business and then rebrand it once we became bigger.

Liquid Logistics still exists as a brand. We take people sea-kayaking, from beginner level up to intermediate and really help them to get the skills to be self-sufficient so they can then join a club and do these things themselves.

But I've actually always wanted to add great value and I've got scribblings from 10 years ago where I was looking at building a personal development course and a mindfulness programme.

And back in pre-pandemic March 2020 New Forest Activities was at a point where it was relatively self-sufficient. I had an office manager, a senior instructor doing my marketing, and we had developed the systems and processes.

So, I was ready to begin a new journey, which was to move into helping other business owners, other entrepreneurs, and effectively become a coach, which I'd been putting off!

But then I very much needed to go back to New Forest Activities to help that business because it was losing a great deal of revenue. It presented a challenge that needed to be addressed. And I couldn't leave that to my team alone.

Now I've got a bit of a balancing act between coaching and supporting and working with my team at New Forest Activities and looking to grow my coaching network and my influence to produce resources that are going to help others.

Stephen: Is everybody cut out to start their own business? How would you know whether you're suited? What's your advice?

Sam: That's a very good point because the idea of being an entrepreneur is fashionable. The problem is there's a lot of people selling that idea and a lot of people buying it. They spend four figure sums on a course that promises to propel them to instant riches.

But in the small print it states, 'We do not guarantee these results. They require hard work, dedication, sleepless nights, passion and a real desire to serve'.

It's very easy for these gurus to show examples of people that have made it because people do make it. But it's not for everyone because it does require a certain mindset and execution is the key.

Anybody can have ideas. Ideas, they make the man, but ideas don't make a business. It's the execution, which is important. No matter how many courses you pay for and buy into, unless you're actually going to execute on those ideas, it's not going to work.

Entrepreneurialism is viable. Anybody can do it, but only a few will succeed. You've got to be able to take the knock-backs; you've got to be prepared to fail and fail often. Anybody that's really successful will have failed. They're just prepared to keep going.

I was very fortunate that when I started my journey, I had no commitments whatsoever. I was just out of university. Mum and Dad let me crash in a spare room at the back of their house for a year or so while I set the business up. I didn't have a day off for around two years. But I didn't see it as work. I saw it as play because I had some canoes and I was taking people out for an event.

If you've left a job where you were working a comfortable nine to five and getting a decent wage, you have to be prepared to work hard for not very much money to make it stick. I would always suggest to people that you can turn your passion into income, but it's not going to happen overnight. First you want to do it as a side show. Do it alongside something that is paying the bills, something that is covering what your family needs or covering your mortgage.

Let's say you are a graphic designer. There are now multiple cloud systems and you can put yourself on Upwork and offer your services as a freelancer. Get yourself 20 hours a week, enough to pay the bills.

Make sure you're sorted and then your new business, which you're passionate about, you could do on the side. Because then you will realise whether you want to do it or not.

I am a Paddlesports coach and I love paddling but I have to be very careful not to kill that passion by turning it into a 'job!'

You might be better off just taking a highly paid job to buy the free time that you need to live out your passion.

Stephen: How do you see the future?

Sam: I have an interest in future technology and I'm keen to support start-ups in that space as well. So, my kind of training and coaching is very much aimed at people that are forward-thinking.

I want to leverage my own ideas with my own businesses. I'm currently building a virtual reality project that is going to be a team building and training tool and raising funding for that.

But I also want to show people opportunities and establish businesses that are set up to scale at an exponential rate.

And I'm a member of The Abundance Community

(www.abundance.community).

This is for tech entrepreneurs, investors and operators of businesses in health care, AI and web conferencing software.

The Abundance Community believes that technology is growing at an exponential rate. When I was a kid, we didn't even have computers, just this big box and you could do word processing on it.

Facebook and Google didn't exist 15 years ago and now they're the biggest businesses on the face of the earth.

There are new opportunities now like that.

Lastly, I've set up a Business Support Network on Facebook to try and help other business owners, which is a really useful resource for dealing with the pandemic and discusses showing leadership and being honest.

Stephen: Can you summarise your outlook on life?

Sam: I've been obsessed with personal development, since I was in my teens and was reading the Tony Robbins books when I was 18 or19. Also, I took an NLP (Neuro-Linguistic Programming) course right back at the start and I was using the ropes courses to talk executives through stressful situations. I got these guys at the top of a trapeze pole or a telegraph pole at about 40 feet in the air. Here was me, an 18, 19-year-old, coaching them through the process of being stressed.

One of my own favourite philosophers is the late Alan Watts who said,

'There's no point making plans for the future if you're unable to live in the present. Because no matter how great the future is and no matter how great an experience you create within yourself it's transient, it just passes. If you aren't able to live now and be happy now and be grateful now and content and kind in the present then no future is going to help you, because you're always going to be looking for the next thing'.

And one of the really big lessons that I train my staff to put out is there's things that you can change and things that you can't change.

And when there's something that you can't change going on, it's very easy to get sucked in and be a victim and feel that it's not fair. Why is this happening to me?

But what we can change is our attitude to it and the way we act and behave.

It's all right having ideas and mantras on how to live your life when it's plain sailing. But it's when it actually gets tough that it matters.

When there's a crisis or challenge, people's true selves come out.

Who are the natural leaders? Who are the people that are going to question stuff? Who are the ones that are going to sit back and absorb, who are go getters that are going to get out there and maybe talk it over with others?

And I ensure that the information that comes into me is positive, following the idea that you're the total of the five people with whom you spend time.

And I've four core attitudes that I try and cultivate in myself and encourage others to embrace.

The first one is gratitude. Gratitude is based on what has happened and what we have now. I am grateful for the meal I had last night, the roof over my head. The fact that I'm healthy and able to speak to you now.

The second is that you are really passionate about what you do. You can be a cleaner in a hospital, who is passionate about their role because they don't see themselves as cleaner rather than someone who talks to and helps the patient.

Somebody might deem that menial but actually it's very important because it's the talking and the conversation with the patients that is helpful.

The third attitude is responsibility for everything that happens to you. I am acting as if I create my own reality and respond accordingly. I create the things that happen to me. I'm responsible for how people react and respond as well.

The final attitude is kindness. I want to show kindness to the world. If someone comes at you aggressively if you put kindness back at them, it's very hard for them to remain angry. Be kind and appreciate that if you were in that person's shoes, if you had their entire backstory and their entire life experiences, could you have done anything different?

And I use mindfulness to observe myself and that's why mindfulness is my overall tool. If you catch yourself in a state where you're angry, stressed or anxious, examine the four attitudes.

Are you taking responsibility for this situation? Are you being passionate? Are you grateful for what you have? And are you showing kindness? It's the practice of meditation, the practice of mindfulness that allows you to catch yourself. The real secret sauce is that ability to observe how you are acting out. Because we're all human.

We are emotional creatures. But mindfulness practice allows you to catch yourself.

You think to yourself, 'Isn't it interesting that person triggered that emotion or that situation triggered that emotion?'

And through practice, you can get that down from being angry for an hour to maybe 30 minutes. And maybe if you get really good at it, you can catch yourself in the moment. And maybe you can just be angry for just a few moments and then let it go.

That's how I like to live my life.

I can almost hear the excitement in Sam's voice as he describes how he used the pandemic to progress his own ideals.

Because of the pandemic he has to focus more on his original enterprise, whilst expanding his network and accelerating his plans to be a coach, the new modern name for a guru!

And in this context, he shares his philosophy and love of mindfulness techniques.

It's quite clear that Sam wants to be a powerhouse in the world of personal development and I suspect he will be very successful!

11

Marcus Watson

Co-Founder and CEO, Adoreum Partners

www.adoreum.com

I have known Marcus for many years, and he is a brilliant example of The Authentic Entrepreneur. Humble, caring and honest and an amazing networker as well as a brilliant businessperson. He actually calls himself The Compassionate Entrepreneur in his LinkedIn profile!

We both have had a similar health crisis, which we have dealt with in our separate ways.

I'll let Marcus tell you his story…

I currently run Adoreum which started over 11 years ago as a business development consultancy that I set up with Rob Hersov.

At that time, I was raising money for early-stage media, technology and hospitality companies but this was just post Lehman Brothers and that had all stopped.

Rob and I both had internet companies back then in the mid to late nineties and when we got reintroduced, he originally tried to hire me to run a business that his wife had set up, which I didn't want to do.

But Rob introduced me to a guy who was creating event platforms for NetJets in New York. Rob had just sold his private aviation business, Marquis Jets, to NetJets and had become Vice Chairman.

So, Rob and I decided to replicate this business in Europe, the Middle East and Africa. We were creating event platforms and business development strategies, which brought together interesting business leaders, investors, entrepreneurs and high net worth individuals. Rob has this incredible network and this phenomenal ability to introduce people and create value and friendships through those introductions.

He said, 'You do all the hard work and run it and I'll be Chairman and put my network in!'

But at the time, a bit like today, the economy was struggling, and it was difficult to get deals done.

So we launched Adoreum as a strategic and business development consultancy and over the years we worked for brands and every variant of luxury, lifestyle, and financial services, including automotive, private members clubs, aviation, watch, jewellery, hedge funds, wealth managers, private banks and charities, creating interesting, engaging, authentic events to which we would invite our friends. These were great business development platforms.

Rob and I started investing in early-stage businesses very early into the Adoreum journey and we helped those businesses in the same way that we helped our other clients using our network, experience and expertise.

After exiting a few of the companies we were shareholders in we decided that going forward we didn't want to work for big companies anymore. We only wanted to work for companies we were investing in and we were helping to start. So that's where we are today.

And we wanted to keep that network going. We all love people and the authentic relationships we create and nurture.

You get to meet fantastic people that you wouldn't typically get to meet in the course of running a business. We wanted to keep that going because that was the platform through which we had fun. We develop amazing friendships. We raise money for the charities that we support, and we find interesting businesses in which to invest.

We think of it as an international members club for High Net Worth Individuals, business leaders, philanthropists, investors, academics and creative visionaries who believe in the power of a diverse collective to influence for good.

The other side of what we do is led by my business partner and Chairman David Tabizel. It's Adoreum Capital where we back great entrepreneurs coming up with interesting ideas and also start businesses with talented management. A particular focus at the moment is in the genomics sector.

I'm an investor in 20 or so different businesses and the Adoreum platform helps all of those businesses by using our network, the events and our collective experience.

Stephen: That's very inspiring. Now can you tell us about your journey to get there?

Marcus: My dad is an entrepreneur. He set up his construction business when I was two years old. For me being an entrepreneur was never alien.

My Dad had nothing to help him start the business. He did have a guy who backed him but there was no family money at all. But I wanted to diversify the family away from being reliant solely on the construction business which is sensitive to all the kinds of economic cycles.

When I was at university, I was buying and selling things with friends. I found I just loved the sale. I still do. I love raising money for a project or when one of them wins a contract using our network and relationships.

So, I had an attraction to business very early on and when I left university, which again was in a recession in 1994, I had my bachelor's degree in biology but went on to a Master's in International Business Management at King's College in London because I wanted to learn about financial markets. I didn't know anything about them. And I thought, well, that would be a fantastic grounding for business.

Then I worked for a private merchant bank called Duncan Lawrie and there I realised that I loved people and I loved selling. Then I worked for a couple of guys from within the bank who set up their own business, which is now called Sigma Capital plc.

But I realised pretty quickly that investment banking wasn't for me. I just didn't like the environment. It wasn't collaborative and I knew that the time was right to do my own thing.

I left and formed an internet company back in the mid to late nineties with a friend of mine, Dave Wardlaw and backed by a wonderful guy, Sir Harry Solomon.

That was an incredible learning process because the industry was moving so quickly so we found it very easy to raise money because a lot of people were interested in deploying capital into internet businesses.

We made loads of mistakes, met lots of interesting people, built a business that we eventually sold called Kitbag.com. And that was an accelerated real life, hands-on, feet to the fire MBA!

Then I knew I was always going to be an entrepreneur and there was no way I was going back into banking or working for a big company.

I knew that wasn't going to make me happy. But I also knew that I had to work really hard to try and be successful.

I think a lot of that drive came from the fact that I was very sick as a kid. I was diagnosed with a condition called Crohn's Disease, which is an auto-immune disease.

When I was 11, I was admitted to Great Ormond Street Hospital where they diagnosed it. I was quite a sickly child and I had my first major operation at 15. I missed out on my formative teenage years but I was driven by the fact that I had this condition because I knew I could get really sick at any moment, which I did over the course of the years.

I thought when I'm fit and healthy, I need to work like crazy. I need to make some capital because I'm going to have to look after myself and my family. And what happens if my dad's business goes bust? I'll have to look after them as well.

I am a massive worrier. I'm getting better but I'm still anxious. So that was the thing that drove me. I now call it my Super Power!

For many, many years I'd disregarded my Crohn's disease. I didn't want to talk about it because it's an embarrassing disease to have. But it did really drive me.

And then I met an amazing guy called Rick Parfitt Jnr, son of the late Rick Parfitt of Status Quo.

He's an Ambassador for Crohn's and Colitis UK. He said it was really important to tell people that have the condition that they can lead a normal life. So, I want to go out, tell young people that having Crohn's disease, having ulcerative colitis, doesn't mean you can't be successful in life. It doesn't mean you can't have business success, get married, have kids.

Stephen: Interestingly, something like that can set your life on such a positive trajectory.

But moving ahead, how do you spot authentic people because you are a master at it and you've also had your ups and downs? I think it's quite important to be able to spot people that are going to support you and people that are not.

Marcus: The most important criteria for me no matter whether it's someone in my personal life, a potential friend or business, is that if I don't believe that they're kind and compassionate then I know they're not for me.

I only really want to bring people close to me who are kind and compassionate. I was very lucky in business early on. I met some amazing people even though I had a terrible boss in my first job who wasn't kind and compassionate at all!

But my next boss, Graham Barnett, was a very hard businessman, but he's kind and compassionate and he was always great to me. And we're still friends.

Then I met Sir Harry Solomon, who was one of the main investors in the internet company I co-founded. And he's an incredibly kind man, with absolute integrity. They're the sorts of people that I want to be in business with.

But I've learnt over the past few years that there are people in this world whom I suspect qualify as psychopaths. They are very good at giving the impression that they are kind and compassionate when they are actually the opposite.

So, although I think I'm very good at spotting kind authentic people, I'm still very wary because I've had some really bad experiences with people who are brilliant at covering up the fact that they're actually not very nice.

Those people are quite difficult to spot but I do think you get better at it as you grow older.

And I've got a really tight-knit group of friends in business. People like you and David Tabizel, Sneh Khemka, Dominic McVey and Andy Thomas. and also, my best friends from school, Berni, Sean, Randal and Srin. And my family are incredibly important to me. My Dad is my hero, and my wife and children are also best friends. They're very smart as well as kind.

The most important thing if you want to be a successful entrepreneur, is obviously that you have to be prepared to work really hard. You have to be prepared to go above and beyond what is considered the normal kind of effort you put into work.

You know, I trained myself, around about the time I set up Adoreum, to get up at five o'clock in the morning just to get more done. There's no substitute for it. If you run your own business, you've got to be prepared to work super hard. Not always, because the other benefit of working for yourself and being an entrepreneur is you can take time out. When you build a business to a scale where you have people who can run it, you don't have to worry so much.

The other thing is to be kind and compassionate to people. This will stand you in good stead in the long term. You will get hurt, of course, and you will come across bad people. You will have some challenging periods during your entrepreneurial journey. But if you're kind and compassionate and you're fair and authentic you'll come through it and you'll come through it stronger. You'll have some fantastic business partners and most importantly you'll be at peace with how you got there.

You'll be a lot happier at the end of that journey or once you've achieved some success.

Marcus had his Crohn's disease from a youngster and that helped him focus on building businesses because at no point could he be certain when he would be well or ill. That uncertainty drove him forward.

In my case, I had colon cancer mid-way through my career which took me out of the system for around 2 years. I used that experience to stop, reflect and change, because by then my sons were becoming self-supporting, I had made a modest amount of money and I wanted to escape the corporate environment I had re-entered once I had sold my business. Adversity can be an important time to rise to the challenge.

Another point Marcus mentioned is spotting the psychopaths. The smooth talker who really has only their interests at heart. I remain not very good at spotting these characters even after years of 'training' but in every case, I've found that had I done due diligence on them before becoming involved, it would have saved me energy and money!

Lastly, the question of having to work hard comes up again. It's my view that the drive to put in the hours comes from the passion for what you're doing. I did put in the hours, but I rarely thought I was working hard. It was mainly, but not always, fun!

It's always a joy speaking to Marcus. His enthusiasm is infectious and he's always there with a creative solution to any perceived setback.

12

Sir Harry Solomon

Entrepreneur, Philanthropist, Mentor, Investor

Sir Harry, after several decades in business, decided to concentrate on helping others. He and I were 'meant to' meet and we had been on each other's radar a long time.

He invested in one of Marcus Watson's television start-ups Pulse Films, his PA, Debby, is a long-standing friend and she also happens to be Asher's Mum!

Furthermore, for many years I lived around the corner from his office in Hampstead, London.

It, therefore, was a great pleasure to finally meet him, albeit via Zoom, and conduct this interview.

To start at the beginning, I qualified as a solicitor in 1960 and practiced law for 15 years. For the first few years, I practiced Criminal work and defended many criminals.

After that, I joined a large firm and did Commercial and Conveyancing transactions. I became very friendly with David Thompson, a client of mine in the meat business.

In 1974 David approached me about setting up a new food business together. He said there were a lot of opportunities in that sector and he thought that together we could do very well.

Whilst nervous about a new career, it seemed an excellent opportunity as I was not committed or dedicated to law. I, therefore, left practice and in 1975 we started our business Hillsdown Holdings.

Over the years we acquired many companies, some of them from receivership and often companies that were performing badly.

What we found in most companies, including those that had failed, was that the top management was often poor, but there were many others in middle management and lower down the scale, who were excellent.

They knew the business well, they wanted to give more to the business, but no-one had ever encouraged them or brought them on.

We found that if one could unlock the potential of these people, the businesses were often revived and became very successful. The company grew very quickly, went public in the early '80s and became a member of the FTSE 100. We had companies in many different countries and we were one of the biggest food manufacturers in Europe.

We supplied most of the major supermarkets and were very large suppliers to Marks and Spencers, Sainsbury's and Tesco. We specialised in the supermarket's own label sales.

I was the Joint Chairman and Chief Executive of the business and was working extremely hard and travelling a lot. In 1990 I decided that I needed to change direction and brought in a new Chairman – a Chief Executive had already been appointed – and I embarked on a new career.

This really involved backing younger people and making investments in their businesses. Again, trying to find the right young people and unlocking their potential.

At the same time, together with Sir Ronald Cohen, we founded The Portland Trust which has offices in London, Tel Aviv and Ramallah and is involved in trying to encourage a Two-State solution for the Palestinians and Israelis and helping the Palestinians economically.

For many years, we have had a family Charitable Trust and the Trustees are my Wife and three children. I have five Grandchildren and as each one of them reaches the age of 23 they are invited to become Trustees of the Charitable Trust and two of them have already done that. Every Trustee is asked to champion and sponsors a particular charity or cause, which is dear to them and be responsible for it. We meet quarterly and take our donations very seriously.

I believe it is important to try and secure some sort of balance in life between work and leisure and this is very difficult when

The Authentic Entrepreneur

you are building and running a big business. One always has to make compromises and often family life suffers. I suppose this is inevitable, but it is important to try and balance what you do. I believe that exercise is very important and it has certainly been a real benefit to me in keeping physically and mentally fit over the years.

Stephen: What would you advise a young entrepreneur starting out today in the context of the fact that I have noticed that being an entrepreneur these days is quite fashionable and of course with the Pandemic there will be a lot of people out of work as well, but I don't believe everybody should be looking to start their own business, do you?

Harry: Many people want to start their own business and many people try and fail. It is extremely difficult to build a business from scratch and I think there are some necessary ingredients.

First, you have to have real passion and belief in the business you want to build. Second, you must be prepared to work extremely hard and make sacrifices. Third, you have to have good people around you and certainly someone who is numerate and understands the financial position and control of the business. Fourthly, you will always need more money than you think and it will always take longer than you think to succeed.

Having said all of that, if it becomes really clear that the business is not going to work, cut it — too many people hope things will get better and they get more and more into debt when a hard-headed look at the business would have made it clear it was never going to succeed.

An entrepreneur should not be frightened of failure and must have the courage to try again with another opportunity. Often the problem with entrepreneurs is that they have great ideas, they are visionaries and very bright, but have no idea how to run a business. They need good people alongside them.

I believe that success and failure in any business is all about people. You can have a very average business, that will really shine with good management running it, but the same average business will fail with poor management. Motivation, teamwork and enthusiasm are essential in any business.

Stephen: Lastly when you take over a company, what do you do when the culture of the acquired company is nothing like yours?

Harry: Many of the companies we bought at Hillsdown had a completely different ethos from ours and we had to make fundamental changes. One has to stamp one's own authority on the business but to do this by persuasion and example.

Stephen: Thank you very much Sir Harry – do you have any parting words?

Harry: If you ask me what I think one's ambition in life should be, it is contentment, which is often very difficult to achieve. It doesn't mean any lack of ambition, but it means being content with your lot in life.

Sir Harry is a wonderful example of practicing what he preaches. I have known a couple of people he has backed and he also suggested donating royalties to The Prince's Trust and made the necessary introductions.

I can only hope that by following his example, I too can reach a comparable state of contentment!

Part 3: Your Authentic Business Journey

This book is not intended as a business manual.

Business manuals have their place, but once you put what you learn into practice, it becomes real experience and that knowledge becomes wisdom.

In this book, I want to spell out a few of the things I have learnt on the way but they are pointers only and should not be taken as ultimate truths.

Hopefully, they will give you a flavour of how you can run your Authentic Businesses.

You'll find a page at the end of this book which tells you more about the The Prince's Trust, and I encourage you to investigate their work as you might be eligible for one of their programs.

Working for a Company or Becoming your Own Boss?

If you are still set on becoming an entrepreneur you have to get real about the consequences, especially if you are currently employed in a well-paid job in a company that cares for you and grants you a myriad of benefits.

The Bank of England employed one of my oldest friends all his working life. He always seemed rather jealous of me, constantly implying that he doesn't understand how someone like me could make all that money. The fact is that in salary and benefits he was equally remunerated but now also he has the benefit of a generous pension.

The other consideration is the hard work you will probably have to endure, as especially at the beginning you'll be on call 24/7.

There were a few times when I would arrive home in the evening, only to receive a phone call urging me to return to the office. Broadsystem had projects operating continuously and the computer might malfunction, a freelancer not turn up, a water pipe burst. In the beginning, it was all down to me.

But at the same time, it did not feel like work. It was fun and exhilarating. I certainly enjoyed life more than when I had a strict 8:30 am to 5:30 pm routine at the Electricity Council! (Before you ask, the 'working day' back then was longer than 9 am to 5 pm).

You also have to be passionate about the business area you want to enter, because you will likely be focusing on it for three years or longer.

Starting on your own requires a giant leap of faith in yourself. You might be putting your house on the line and you will almost certainly be taking a pay cut at first.

And you could lose everything!

Working for your current company might be giving you 70% of what you want but sap your creativity. Mixing with people who all think the same way does not suit people with big visions and ideas.

But even I would have loved to have been working at Apple alongside Steve Jobs when he invented the iPhone with Jonathan Ives.

Life Not Money

The biggest trap for aspiring entrepreneurs is the belief that money will make them happy and more money will make them happier, even though on some level we all know this to be untrue.

Yet so many successful entrepreneurs define their success by how much money they have made and then they set a new goal.

First £1m, then £100m, then £1billion…

It's easy to understand why.

Money is measurable and you can look every day at your bank balance, but try quantifying your happiness or fulfilment!

Once, whilst on business in Mumbai, I was looking for a synagogue to say prayers for my father who had recently died. And in the Jewish tradition, which I was still following at that time, it is required to offer prayers for a deceased parent, every day for 11 months.

There I was in Mumbai and I asked my contacts if anyone knew the location of a synagogue that would be open early in the morning for prayers. Someone suggested one and my taxi dropped me in a street in the middle of nowhere. There was no sign of a synagogue.

This street was filled with homeless souls who slept on the pavement or if they were lucky, in the water pipes that were being laid. Some were brushing their teeth but I am not sure how they got the water. The strange thing was that they looked clean and the women in their saris were as beguiling as in any City.

I had just arrived from Los Angeles, which is one of the richest cities in the world.

In Los Angeles, some areas were strictly off-limits but here I was in a part of Mumbai which seemed to be inhabited solely by the homeless.

One man came shuffling up to me beaming and asked what I was looking for. My first reaction was to back away especially as some of his mates were looking at me curiously.

But their energy seemed very amicable so I told them that I was looking for the synagogue.

I admit that at the back of my mind I was concerned that a Jew looking for a synagogue in Mumbai might not be the commonest sight!

They explained that the synagogue had closed down a year before my visit and then described where I should go to find a service. They helped me hire a taxi to take me there, explaining to the driver where I should be dropped off.

This was a salutary tale because it showed me that you can still be penniless AND happy. (Not that I am advocating this!)

Those people were only too happy to help. Nor, did they ask for money in return.

So out of the challenge of finding the synagogue my life was enriched.

We all indeed need a baseline level of capital to keep us comfortable but true happiness then comes from other places like community, supportive friends, good health, and interesting life experiences.

And as a life-long meditator, I would also add contentment and peace of mind.

By way of example, I'll always remember a lesson I learnt when I first made a significant amount of money.

My first ventures were successful but it was only really when I had sold Broadsystem and was on a profit share that I achieved a level of comfort financially and although I was of course grateful every time I made a financial gain, the difference it made to my life diminished.

Mid-career my shares in Shine TV had been sold. And I was sitting in Maison Bertaux, one of the few old-style cafes left in London's Soho, waiting for my bank to tell me that my money had arrived in my account.

I was trying to feel excited.

It was the most money that I had ever made but I actually did not NEED it.

I was musing, 'what can I do with this money?' And I thought 'I will buy a flat by the seaside'. And I tried to get excited about buying the flat.

Excitement came, but I was not exactly euphoric.

And a guy was sitting next to me with his family saying to his wife, 'Oh, I forgot to go to the cash machine. We've got no cash,' and Maison Bertaux did not take cards!

So, I leaned over to their table. 'Excuse me, I've just made quite a lot of money unexpectedly and I would like to treat you to tea'.

The guy looked at me suspiciously and replied,

'No, we're alright, thanks.'

My mood instantly collapsed because my help had been spurned and I felt rejected.

It showed me how volatile our emotions can be because in all honesty at that moment, treating that family would have given me the same pleasure, if not more, than the transitory uplift from seeing my bank balance.

On a more positive note, for a few years, we had a financial interest in a yoga and community centre in Bali. Nobody knew we were involved there, yet strangers would approach us with congratulations because they could sense that we had some involvement in the enterprise. There was obviously a glow of satisfaction surrounding us!

You go through various stages in life. Youth, adolescence, middle age, and elder statesman. As an entrepreneur, you'll hopefully reach a place where you can make a real difference and learn that satisfaction comes from the seeds of your initial actions, and by using the fruit of those actions you can improve other people's lives.

What qualities are necessary?

Paradoxically, or so it might seem, to be a successful entrepreneur you need to show sincere empathy, compassion, and interest in everybody you are in contact with.

I'm a bit of a Jekyll and Hyde in that I can be seen as hard, but actually, I have a heart of gold (honestly!). Only today, Luiza called me an Unhinged Genius, which I think broadly describes many entrepreneurs!

But I am genuinely interested in people and their stories and whenever I meet someone for the first time, I want to know all about them. This leads me to quite naturally asking what society would term indiscrete questions but I have found over the years people find this quite endearing.

This is a strategy I have naturally used time and again in my business dealings. Paul Boross makes the point very eloquently that if you use empathy and humour in a meeting, people will want to do business with you.

Silence is Golden

Empathy can include just listening carefully.

A couple of years ago, I was asked to intervene in a dispute between two companies who were in a joint venture.

They had reached an impasse and a meeting had been arranged in Los Angeles to try and resolve the situation.

I knew one of the parties well, but not the other. One of the founders of the other company lived near where we were staying and I agreed to attend providing he gave me a lift to the meeting.

When he first picked me up, he was quite wary, assuming I had a hidden agenda and I was just there to garner intelligence for the other side.

But I explained that there was nothing in it for me and I was just attending to help both parties achieve a reconciliation.

Gradually he relaxed and began to relate his back story and I just listened sympathetically, whilst saying nothing.

Suddenly he had an idea. A breakthrough. Maybe he could suggest a new way of compromising? He outlined his thinking and asked for my feedback. It sounded great to me and I encouraged him to suggest his idea at the meeting.

At the office, there was a slight air of tension, but I confessed that there might be a breakthrough idea and asked the chap to explain.

I could see the amazement on the faces of everyone and a deal was done then and there.

The meeting finished quickly and the company that initially invited me contacted me later to thank me for MY brilliant idea. Well, I emphasised I really had nothing to do with it other than being a good listener - but they didn't believe me!

Timing is Everything

Rarely do new companies hit the market at exactly the right time and place.

I thought about setting up a precursor to Skype at least a year before Skype appeared. We even had an operational test service and I touted the idea of putting telecom operators out of business. The issue was how to monetise this ground-breaking new idea. I simply didn't have an answer, and I gave up. Yet Skype was sold to Microsoft for $8.5 billion!

Broadsystem worked with major newspapers for phone-in astrology and racing results and television companies for competitions.

When I was starting, I cannot tell you how many people said they would never ring into a TV program. Truth be told, neither would I BUT a hell of a lot of people did!

So, you have to be at the right time and place and be able to see the future. With cable TV, I saw a trend, but my timing was wrong. I was too early and it took a decade for it to really take off.

This timing thing is tricky and is a skill you have to cultivate through experience. Even the brilliant Steve Jobs built what could be called a prototype iPhone called the Newton, but it was a commercial failure.

And if you do fail sometimes, as Jobs did then, merely treat it as feedback that will help you fine-tune your commercial acumen.

And I will always remember attending one of the first Internet conferences. Someone asked the 'expert' on stage whether the Internet would be used for television streaming. The answer came, 'There will never be enough bandwidth!'

If I had not been engrossed with Broadsystem at that time, I would have immediately set up an internet TV venture – but even then, it would have been many years before it would have been commercially successful. It's one thing to see the future and quite another to monetise it at the right time.

Business Plan

When I started out, I had never done a business plan.

Luckily, a private investor in Cable London had a large Accountancy practice and one of his staff produced my plan. As it was such a large project and we only had very limited comparable data from cabled American cities, the whole enterprise was a leap of faith but we still had no trouble getting backing because the rewards were perceived to be so enormous. As there was no satellite TV and no Internet streaming, we assumed we would have an ongoing monopoly on multi-channel TV. How things have changed!

By the time it came to finance Broadsystem, I had learnt that many first-time entrepreneurs raise much less than they really need due to lack of experience or confidence or over-optimistic business projections.

They will raise a hundred thousand pounds for a business that clearly requires half a million pounds. They run low on funds because they did not meet their own sales projections. Or as in my own case, I underestimated the number of staff needed to handle an unexpected increase in clients and decreased profit margins due to competition.

By the time you have launched and need more money, it can be too late. New funders will want much better terms or a 'Saviour' might buy the company at a knocked-down price.

But with Broadsystem it was a much smaller proposition financially than Cable London, with potentially immediate rewards.

Yet I knew instinctively, that whatever the projections, we needed to get the initial funding level right.

We set out to raise £250,000, which in 1983 was a lot of money. Melvin, my accountant, ensured the plan showed we needed £200,000 with £50,0000 contingency.

Given that the soon to be closed BT Guideline services were receiving 300 million calls annually, we felt pretty comfortable with our figures.

But before going further, I wanted to see whether I would be able to attract a broadcasting partner. Luckily, I had an intermediary who knew high-ups in the BBC and arranged a very productive meeting with the then Head of the BBC's commercial subsidiary, BBC Enterprises.

He was kind enough to write me a letter of support confirming they would be open to experimenting with interactive TV.

Our business plan predicted that it would take a couple of years to break even and we would be making significant but not extraordinary profits after three or four years. This would enable the backers to sell the business and make a return of three to five times their funding.

We intended to sell the business from the outset because we knew outside investors would expect an exit plan. Therefore, in the plan, we identified future potential suitors.

Jason explained that his initial investors were interested only in the exit even though he had no plans to sell it. Therefore, in his second company, he attracted those who were equally interested in helping him achieve his aspirations for growing the business.

Of course, shareholders can be paid dividends from ongoing profits – providing there are any. And choices have to be made between retaining profits for future company growth, distributing them, or retaining them for unexpected calamities – like a pandemic.

I should emphasize that neither Gaelle, Toby, Aron nor Asher have any plans to bring in outsiders and are content with Organic growth – literally in Gaelle's case!

Paul Boross is an island unto himself, and successfully partners with others as and when necessary.

Bernard and Marcus have turned their friends into investors, who seem to be happy to journey with them and enjoy the ride.

The Board

With Broadsystem, as well as Cable London, I needed to form a Board that would give a backer confidence we had enough business experience between us.

Many backers have a supply of trusted business people who they place in the Chair role of their investments. In this instance, however, my eventual backer 3i was happy with my mentor, Jerrold Nathan.

I also put my accountant Melvin Kay, on the Board, as well as Malcolm Gee, who had helped me put together my cable franchise bids.

Looking back, I should have also found someone with media contacts because although my Board members had 'traditional' business experience, they found it difficult to cope with the way I thought as a visionary! I had a very clear idea that my interactive publishing business would be able to generate significant revenue but my colleagues were more sceptical.

'We will put in a few thousand pounds and the best of luck to you!'

And that was about the limit of their exposure. One invested £10,000 and made £250,000 and another invested twice as much with twice the return. He bought a second home with that, which he named Broadsystem!

Raising Funds

Before raising funds, you need to have a vision, do a viable plan, decide your co-Directors, and see if you can test your plan in the marketplace.

I did this by getting a letter of intent from the BBC saying that they would support us. I then raised enough funding with the contingency should the business be slower to take off than planned.

At this stage, you have to decide whether you are going to get the money from your savings, mortgaging your house, in a friends and family fundraising, or from external investors like Angels and private equity funds, crowd-funding, trade investors or a combination.

Obviously, each method has advantages and disadvantages and the best place to start is to imagine what would happen if everything went wrong and how you might feel about that.

The pitfalls of obtaining money from friends and family are pretty obvious. Emotions are involved anyway and if things go wrong these are heightened.

Of course, if you are involved in a family business, there is always the risk of invoking a family feud. It's therefore a pleasure to see how well Mario and Asher get on with each other as do Jason and Karen Kirk.

And another growing method is crowd-funding, but I am definitely not an advocate unless you are perhaps marketing a product with a huge fan base. Nor do I like the smaller public markets like AIM in the UK.

The issue with both crowd-funding and AIM is that you can end up with thousands of small investors who can only imagine the upside and are less than understanding when things go awry. Nor do they necessarily have follow-through capital. They will invest once but you will be lucky if they put in further funds.

AIM also had additional costs and you are completely beholden to market forces that are sometimes disengaged from the actual company performance.

My preferred investors are therefore Angels, trade, and private equity.

The number of Angels seems to have grown exponentially in recent years. These are professionals, who one way or another, have been successful in their own right and want to help others succeed by investing in promising start-ups.

Sir Harry Solomon, epitomises the ideal Angel.

They will often have sufficient funds to follow through if they are minded to.

With Angels, the absolute necessity is to undertake due diligence. Where have they invested before, what is their reputation and how is their judgement rated and how have they supported a founder when things have not gone as planned?

There are many Angel clubs and events and I recommend looking at initiatives such as Seedcamp, Founders Forum, and GrowthDeck, where you will find a variety of both private equity and Angels.

Meeting potential investors in a Seedcamp conference also allows you to check them out and vice versa.

Approaching private equity companies requires research to understand which industries are their focus and primarily if they would back a start-up. Although I did not myself use an intermediary to raise funds, these days you might be best advised to talk to ones like Clarity or Ironbridge Capital Partners.

When raising money for my own business I was open to finding a trade partner, so as well as speaking to 3i, I also approached one of the commercial broadcasting companies, TVS, which had the TV licence for the South of England.

TVS expressed preliminary interest but I had a firm offer from 3i and progressing discussions with TVS would have meant holding that investment up which I was reluctant to do, so I accepted the 3i deal.

Had TVS progressed, they might have helped speed up our entry into mass TV interaction.

But it does raise the important point of whether you should involve trade partners at the business inception. My own feeling is that it depends entirely on the terms.

Many trade partners invest on the understanding that if you receive an offer to buy your business, they would have the right to match it. Others ask for a majority stake or a minimum of 26% for tax purposes.

Too many restrictions and you end up working for the trade investor by default and selling to them at a significant discount.

But personally, I am open to involving trade investors provided they help ensure the business will have a greater chance of success.

When I was on the Board of Shine TV, one of the investors was Sony, but News Corporation ultimately bought the company and everybody was happy with the deal.

If you have a potential trade investor opportunity, I would look at that seriously because it might accelerate the growth of your enterprise.

My approach when starting out was to hedge my bets by compromising on the size of my shareholding to ensure that no matter what happened I wouldn't be homeless and penniless!

Many entrepreneurs baulk at giving away a majority stake but back then I hadn't built a successful track record and so I had to compromise.

Moreover, at the point of the Broadsystem fundraising, Cable London was simply eating up money to dig up roads and there was absolutely no guarantee it would be a viable business.

Which relates back to my earlier point. With cable, we won five London Boroughs requiring multiple fund-raising exercises and millions of pounds of investment. I made a couple of hundred thousand pounds myself out of the whole enterprise when a media group eventually acquired the company but at each additional fund-raising my own shareholding was diluted.

I subsequently learnt that the way around this is to ensure you own a special class of 'Founder shares' that could be protected from dilution.

I actually had these in Cable London but nobody reminded me at the time I left the company – see Reading The Paperwork below!

Nevertheless, had I been in America, I would probably be a billionaire by now, assuming my company had been Manhattan Cable not Cable London, which leads us to…

Geographical Location

If you're young and mobile, it's always worth considering setting up your enterprise overseas. In some territories there might be tax benefits, others it's the cost of living, labour, and the weather.

Aron seems very content with Bali, as does Toby in Ibiza. In Toby's case, he had a longing to return to the idyllic home of his childhood but for Aron, it was the chance opportunity of working for a Balinese charity.

Most of my extended family emigrated to the States and my son Simon is now a U.S citizen in New York because he considered the opportunities there to be vastly more than in the U.K.

I have set up enterprises in the UK, States, India, Australia, and France and invested in a business in Bali. Following these experiences, I would now just stick to my home country, the UK, because I understand the market and laws so much better.

But if you are adventurous and can arrange a work visa (good luck with that!), the States has a more entrepreneurial approach than in the UK and it is easier to raise funds.

As an example, David McCourt, started off in the States as a prison probation officer and became a cable billionaire. I recommend his book Total Rethink, which gives his perspective.

Reading the Paperwork

I was young, innocent, and trusting when I set up my cable company and I expected everyone involved to protect me. For this reason, I did not give close attention to the numerous legal agreements that were drawn up, especially as applied to myself. But as the company grew larger, I stepped down from an executive function and became a Non-Executive Director.

After about 10 years I was not really that involved and was asked to resign. But about 3 years after my resignation, I discovered that by resigning, I had actually relinquished my Founder shares as outlined in the shareholder agreement! I had not read the agreement because I assumed that the Board would have protected my best interests as Founder.

By resigning, I had actually given up about £500k and not a single colleague had alerted me to this. I learnt that I should have negotiated a mutually agreeable exit and used an employment lawyer to negotiate for me.

You can imagine that this experience made me quite sad and from then on, I resolved to always point out the downsides of any deal I was proposing to others. In this way, I engendered trust, which was great for repeat business.

Due Diligence

I also realised that within the business world there are negative forces and you have to be ever diligent, however Authentic you are. I learnt that not everybody acts as you do.

Always check people out thoroughly before getting involved with them. This is a lesson it took me many years to learn because I always want to see the best in people.

It is industry practice to sign an NDA (Non-Disclosure Agreement) when sharing confidential information especially if you've never dealt with an individual or company before. Any lawyer would draw one up for you and they are particularly relevant if your idea is novel.

But now that I have established a network of trusted contacts, I don't normally bother with one myself.

In the pandemic, many businesses were unable to pay their rents and there were some wonderful stories about the generosity of certain landlords. For example, several Nightingale Hospitals were set up in a venture between the private sector and the NHS and the respective landlords were generous and in almost all cases allowed the hospitals to operate for a period rent-free.

But in other instances, some unscrupulous landlords were totally uncompromising and would rather evict a tenant than accept a lower rent.

These particular landlords were well known for their lack of humanity and a prospective tenant could have checked them out before signing a lease.

My friend Mike Abrahams gave me initial office space, but then he sold his business and as I didn't have a formal rental agreement, the new owner promptly asked me and my staff to leave.

I staggered into the street outside and opposite there was a 'For Rent' sign on a large, attractive warehouse. I wandered in and found the landlord in an outbuilding overlooking the Grand Union Canal.

His face was familiar because he had played a part in the Robin Hood TV series.

He showed me around the massive warehouse, and sensing my desperation, insisted I had to take on the whole building or no deal.

What could I do?

I signed the lease, moved my staff into the building, and set about renting out the majority to independent TV producers who all wanted to work in trendy Camden.

At the end of the first quarter, the landlord presented me with our electricity bill and asked for prompt payment. It was £100,000! The rental for the whole building was £75,000

I rang the electricity company, who informed me that the landlord had given them 'our' meter readings explaining that we were using so much electricity because of our computers.

At my insistence, they arranged a meter reader to visit. The landlord was on the fiddle and our bill was around £1,000! Years later, I learnt he had ended up in jail for fraud.

We do not want to think the worst of people and we often do not envisage bad things happening. Very admirable but somewhat unrealistic!

This applies to your potential investors too.

When Broadsystem was growing fast, a property company that wanted to diversify approached me and asked if they could take a stake in my business.

A friend had made the introduction and I could see we could benefit from a cash injection, as I needed to buy equipment for The Daily Mirror racing results service.

At the time of the approach we were doing exceptionally well and we arrived at a price per share as estimated in an independent valuation from an Accountancy firm. But a couple of years later the company's fortunes changed and I thought it wise to sell the business.

Broadsystem's value had diminished and we were offered a price, which would have meant the property company making a loss on their shareholding.

Well, they obviously did not take that kindly and insisted that I paid them back personally for the loss or they would block the sale. As I was financially challenged myself, I had no choice but to accept the offer which I actually thought was quite generous in the circumstances.

I did ask the other shareholders whether they would chip in as they were about to make a substantial return on their initial investment - but they all declined. So, I had to stump up all the money from my 'winnings'.

Ironically, shortly after the sale closed the property company went bust! I have to confess a certain degree of schadenfreude. But my financial contribution for their shares was irrecoverable. And if Broadsystem had not been sold I might have been dealing with their Administrators who would have inherited their shareholding. Trust me - you would not ever want to be dealing with Administrators.

Administrators of a failed company are always first in line to get paid from whatever cash is left in that company. Therefore, they have a vested interest in dragging things out as they are paid by the hour...

Anyway, had I done my due diligence properly, I would never have had them as a shareholder because a property company has a completely different mentality to a media company.

In another salutary episode, when I signed the deal with the Daily Mirror to run their racing results service, I desperately needed more computer equipment fast to handle all the calls and that equipment was out of stock indefinitely.

I knew if we couldn't handle the calls, we'd be up the creek and lose the contract. But then I was tipped off that a competitor with exactly the right amount of computer power was for sale. It was the biggest deal I'd ever done and I had raised funds from the property company so we had enough funds to pay the asking price.

We undertook all the legal work and a date was set for completion of the deal.

Curiously the seller, let's call him Ray, insisted we meet at his lawyers at night, and even more suspiciously he did not turn up but sent one of his lieutenants to represent him.

Without prior warning, the lieutenant produced a new document for me to sign. Apparently, the equipment was leased and money was still owed and Ray had personally guaranteed the repayments. Now Ray wanted me to personally indemnify him in case we defaulted on the lease repayments.

Well at that moment, just before midnight, I should have walked away from the deal but I was too tired to think rationally even though the whole thing was obviously a set-up. And I signed. Only the next day did I realise I was personally guaranteeing Ray around £850,000 should my company go bust.

In an amusing sequel, Ray wanted to thank me for taking this company off his hands and invited me and Lesley to the posh Cipriani Hotel in Venice on holiday with him and his wife. All at his expense.

As Ray was in publishing, I told him I had just been offered the chance to produce the This Morning magazine for Granada TV and they insisted it should be a weekly publication. He listened to my story intently and tears began to cascade from his eyes.

'What on earth is the matter?' I asked.

We were sitting on the terrace of the hotel in the balmy night air, staring across the lagoon at St. Mark's Square. You couldn't ask for a more beautiful view.

'Well,' replied Ray 'If you go weekly with the magazine, you'll go bust. When you go bust, you'll still owe me almost £1m because of your personal guarantee... And then you'll be homeless because I'll seize your house and sell it to recoup my money'.

'You could always let me off?' I replied. Ray was a multi-millionaire.

'Oh, no, I could NEVER do that'.

Ray was absolutely right in that my magazine did fail but I had set aside an amount I could afford to lose and as soon as we had spent that we closed it down. Broadsystem did begin to repay the lease and after a couple of years, we refinanced without the need for my personal guarantee and subsequently paid for the equipment in full.

When mentioning due diligence, people ask if there is a list of questions that they should put to a potential investor, staff member, etc. It is much more usual for an employer to take references on a potential employee, but for other partners such as private equity, trade partners, and landlords, it is much less formal. However, even with my employee hires I went through the same process below.

I get introductions to people who have worked with the potential employee or business partner and ideally see that contact for a cup of coffee but sometimes it would have to be a phone call.

After I have established rapport and only then I will ask questions about the person or organisation 'strictly off the record'.

The general issue with formal employee references is that if you write a bad reference you could end up being sued for defamation so the only reliable way forward is to keep it very informal.

Expect the unexpected

One day the police turned up at Broadsystem and began to interview me in the reception area.

'We are here because we are investigating the murder of a British Telecom engineer and he had your phone number in his diary'.

'Can we not discuss this in the Reception area if you don't mind?' I replied.

I took them to a meeting room and asked to see the phone number. Was it my home phone number?

And one detective said, 'We traced the number to this building. It was 0898 100 100'.

I tried to suppress a smile. After all, they were investigating a murder. I replied, 'That's actually a racing results service'.

They look puzzled so I explained that 0898 100 100 - if they cared to dial it - took callers to our computer to hear racing results!

I led them to our computer room and explained that we had hundreds of thousands of people dialling in every day because the number was promoted by the Daily Mirror. I showed them the relevant page of the newspaper with 0898 100 100 prominently displayed.

Somehow the detectives managed not to look embarrassed and left.

A decade or so later there was a company reunion and one of my former staff members asked loudly if I was still being investigated for murder!

It's kind of funny, but it's also in the category of 'You couldn't make it up!'

Unseen Forces

Being Authentic has to include being aware that there are forces for good and some not so benign.

Tracy probably faces the biggest challenge with the invisible bias in business she finds against women, especially women of colour. But she has used this obstacle to harness her energy and to make the world a better place for all.

But everyone in business has to face the reality of life with all its complications.

Once, I got a call from an American investor who told me he was interested in buying my business. This was years before it was actually for sale. Out of curiosity, I arranged a meeting with the pair representing this American. I did the usual tour and chat and then at the end of the meeting when I thought we had bonded, they asked, 'What do you think of...?'

And they named one of my competitors and I literally said, 'I can't comment on that. You'll have to look at their books'.

An hour later the son of the Founder of the competitor called me.

'Stephen, I'm suing you!' You bad-mouthed us to the Americans and they reported you back to us'.

Yes, it was another set-up! He had clearly sent the Americans to find out all about our business and for good measure threatened to sue me.

I insisted that I had only told them I couldn't comment and that they would have to look at the financial information in the company Accounts, but the son insisted he was taking me to court.

He was Jewish and I was Jewish and it was just a few days before the Jewish New Year and it is traditional to forgive your enemies then.

So, the guy rings me the night before the New Year, forgives me, and drops the lawsuit! Bizarrely, we became friends as a result of this incident. A case of loving your competitors, as Bernard told us.

On another occasion, a guy contacted me wanting, or so he claimed, to interview me for a TV listings magazine but it turned out he was actually on the payroll of yet another competitor!

In a further adventure, a British Telecom contact introduced me to an American publishing company in New York.

I went to meet this company because they wanted to start telephone 'chat lines' in the UK, having experienced major success with them in the States and I had been recommended as a joint venture partner.

The idea was you would chat to your friends on the telephone, at a little over the normal cost, and British Telecom was planning to launch these in the UK. Then they had a change of mind because they realised these could become sex lines.

But I had already signed the joint venture deal with this American company.

Belatedly I did my due diligence only to discover they were running sex lines in the States and realised that Broadsystem was to be their Trojan horse to enter the British marketplace.

I immediately rang my American joint venture partner and told him that I had to pull out of our deal because British Telecom was not proceeding with the chat lines.

Quick as a flash, he announced he was catching the next flight from New York and would be at my office the following morning.

When he arrived, outwardly he was extremely pleasant. Then he said, 'I've come to warn you that if you EVER start a chat lines business without us, you'll be in big trouble and we'll be watching every move you make'.

I knew what that meant.

He finished his coffee and caught a cab back to the airport.

Then I was tipped off that they were a Mafia front company and although they published respectable magazines, they also had a range of sexually explicit titles.

This was another case on my part of not undertaking sufficient due diligence!

Lastly a story of dark forces from Bali…

Once Luiza and I spent a few days in a resort in the unspoilt north of Bali. Most of Bali has now been built on by folk like.. …Well, let's be honest… People LIKE us (not us of course!) and turned into villas.

And in Bali, you don't have to be very rich to be a rich person. For around £100,000 you could build a villa and have staff and grounds.

We were in this ecological hotel and one day we went for a walk and there was an American chap sitting on a wall staring out at the sea and he told us his story.

He said, 'This is my last day in Bali. I'm running away tomorrow. We owned the hotel next to the one you're staying at.

My wife and I came from America to start a new life here, but my wife's mother got sick and we had to return. And we left the hotel in the hands of the manager. He would pay us the profits and obviously keep something for himself. But in the end, the money dried up. We knew the hotel was still functioning so I flew over two years ago to work out what was going on. And when I got to the hotel, I discovered that the manager had gambling debts. He had gambled away all the money.

I tried to fire him, but he replied that I could not do that because he now was the sole owner of the hotel. Not only that, but he was also an Indonesian citizen and I wasn't. But in fact, I had an Indonesian Retirement visa which gave me certain rights.

I hired a lawyer and began legal action to get the hotel returned to my ownership. The trial was coming up and the lawyer asked to meet in private.

I met him in a cafe and the lawyer tells me I have a watertight case, but I'll need to pay him a bribe of an extra $75,000 for the judge!

Luckily, I had befriended a retired police officer. He had seen all sorts of corruption in his day and he told what to do. He asked me to set up a meeting with the lawyer at the Police station.

He instructed me to go to the meeting alleging I had the $75,000 cash and record the conversation.

At the police station, I ensured the lawyer incriminated the judge and then told him the conversation had been recorded and would be sent to the American Consulate who would report him and the judge to the Indonesian Government if they didn't back off.

I left the meeting. The trial went ahead, I won and as soon as I could, I sold the hotel. We completed yesterday and I never want to return to Bali again!'

The moral being that doing business in Paradise-like locations is fine providing you understand the local business culture. I doubt that any amount of due diligence would have foreseen this incident.

Selling

You may feel that you never want to sell your business but life moves on and sometimes it is desirable. A change in life circumstances, trading conditions, and retirement all can be factors.

When selling my business to Rupert Murdoch, I asked him how he intended to motivate me.

He put me on a profit share, which was extremely beneficial and I made a fair amount of money during my three-year earn-out period.

When you sell the business, you will hopefully get a large cheque and consider your options. Again, in some ways, this sounds attractive, but in reality, my experience of those that have sold out, is that after a while you get used to the money and you are itching to do something else. But normally you would be contracted to work for the new owners, for three to four years.

I always counsel people now to consider very carefully before they sell because working again for another company can be soul-destroying.

Asher also makes this point strongly.

Looking back on my own life, my sale to News Corporation was financially beneficial and I met some very interesting people and found myself in some fascinating situations, but I felt rather constrained by the actions I could take, so paradoxically although I had the potential backing of a large corporation behind me, the number of projects that I would have liked to have got involved in was severely curtailed.

And many entrepreneurs, like Bernard, for example, end up buying their original business back. It's often the case that the new owner does not have the same passion as the original Founder. Therefore, often the business underperforms.

What next?

Many of my peers have gone from starting one business to the next. Sometimes it can be in the same field but sometimes I've been amazed at the variety of ventures they have undertaken.

Marcus, for example, seems to have interests in TV production, Adoreum Club, and a recruitment consultancy, as well as being an Advisor to UNICEF.

He, like many others, has a portfolio career and is involved with charities, and sits on boards as a Non-Executive Director – effectively being a mentor in the way Jason describes his Non-Executive Chairman and Director on the Board of KirkandKirk.

Monica has the most extraordinary and varied career both as an intrapreneur and entrepreneur.

Whatever direction you take, the first step will always be the most important. Take your time, do your research, speak to mentors, and most importantly, examine your heart and listen carefully to what it tells you.

But by following your heart, I'm not talking about your emotions. Emotions can take you all over the place! But deep inside there is something that guides you. You may call it intuition, but whatever it is, it won't lead you astray,

Part 4: Go Forth and Prosper!

'The Privilege of a Lifetime is Being Who You Are' Joseph Campbell

Well, we've come to the end of our journey together and I hope you've found it both entertaining, inspirational, and thought-provoking.

The fact that you are here means you ARE Authentic. You don't have to strive at being the best version of yourself – how can you be anything but what you are?

According to the philosopher Joseph Campbell, you begin life from a particular cultural perspective, you reach a stage where perhaps that perspective does not match your own inner beliefs and then you move on through various challenges, ups and downs until you hopefully reach some form of Enlightenment, some peace which transcends the rest of your life.

One of the interesting aspects of Joseph Campbell's philosophy is that life is an adventure and without some form of challenge, be it health, financial, or whatever, we cannot grow as individuals and we cannot experience life to the full.

So, let's look at the various principles that can guide an Authentic Business Life…

Retain the Passion

Don't start anything just for the money!

To be successful and have a fulfilled life, you need to ensure that you are passionate about your business. And if you're not excited every day, find a way out.

Similarly, if you are in business with people you no longer admire 'cut it' as Sir Harry advises or start again as Jason did.

When I carried on working for News Corporation after they acquired my company, I was paid a fortune but felt frustrated and I got very sick. I probably would have become ill anyway, but being unhappy could not have helped.

The moral is to work at ventures that excite you every day and if over the years that passion fades, change direction.

Aron spends some of his time helping stray animals, promoting his passion for veganism, and providing employment and bonding with his suppliers in Bali.

Bali used to have an abundance of skilled craftspeople and artists, but the modern economy has pushed many Balinese into less creative employment. And anything that can be done to help retain these traditional skills, to whatever degree, is helping to maintain traditional Balinese culture.

Toby spreads his knowledge of Ibiza's beauty to thousands of tourists. Before folk like Toby arrived on the island, Ibiza was only known for its nightclubbing. With Toby's mum Sheila, we have been shown hidden bays and vistas, learnt about the fauna, the island's history, and enjoyed Sheila's home-made cakes served with tea of course. I'm not saying which bit of her walk I enjoy most!

And Gaelle, realised in the Dead Sea how natural products can heal the skin and years later when challenged by her daughter Sabrina, set up Gaelle Organic —to use Eco-certified organic ingredients in her cosmetics.

Paul Boross, mentors the head of a charity. He could go and carry some boxes for that charity, but he wants to concentrate on what will help them the most, using his own unique mentoring skills so that his help will trickle down the whole organisation.

And if you're lucky, the enterprise will eventually bring contentment as it did for Sir Harry Solomon.

Finding Your Own Way

It was only when I had a successful business myself and I had a cocktail party for my clients and invited my parents along that my dad confessed how proud he was of me. Because until then I think they thought of me as some sort of renegade who had run off to the Hindu faith and broken away from my own traditions.

Do not expect to be 'understood' by everyone, because by definition your own thought processes will be outside the norm.

This does not mean being obstinate or not listening to contrary views, but weighing them against your own experience and examining your intuition.

Mentorships

You need to build a community of like-minded peers and mentors to support you and give you guidance.

I was lucky because I was at University with Melvin Kay and he was instrumental in supporting my early ventures because of his Accountancy training as well as giving me sound advice.

Then I met Malcolm Gee who was not only another Accountant but became a trusted mentor.

The majority of my extended family live in the States and I visit often. Therefore, when investigating cable TV, I already had contacts and arranged to visit Manhattan Cable to learn about the industry.

But what do you do if you are starting from scratch?

Well, that is one of the reasons why The Prince's Trust exists, so look at their programs. Not only will they take you through business principles, but they will also help you decide whether enterprise is really for you. Also, you will begin to form your own network and might meet someone who becomes a lifelong business partner or mentor.

Sam is a great advocate of The Abundance Network given his interest in technology and he has also founded The Business Support Network on Facebook, which I'm sure he would encourage you to join.

Sam also stresses the need to surround yourself with positive folk on your wavelength.

Do Unto Others

I was surprised when Gaelle informed me that The Talmud, the primary source of Jewish Law, had the Lord asking, 'How did you behave in business?' as the first question after death. The commentary on this explains that how you act in business, defines how you act in life generally.

If you are meant to be an entrepreneur, it is part of your life's purpose and business certainly helped me to become a more fulfilled and rounded individual.

Marcus, deliberately formed the Adoreum Club so that his contacts could meet, enjoy, and perhaps get involved in enterprises together.

Asher is loyal to his early employees, provides English lessons for his staff, and donates to Spread a Smile Charity. Whilst Paul and I literally Spread a Smile through humour!

Sir Harry now devotes his time to philanthropy and investing and mentoring young entrepreneurs.

My philosophy now is to always consider the welfare of your customers, staff, and suppliers equally alongside your own aspirations.

If your customers like the people behind your cash desk because they are genuine, your product delivers its promise and the price is broadly in line with competitors, then they will buy from you again and again.

Destiny

From my own experience, I have long felt that something is guiding my life. I'm happy to accept it may be my subconscious, my genes, or the Divine. I don't know, but I pay attention to it.

My countless coincidences, Toby's revelation on the mountain, Monica's meeting with the MTV founders, Bernard's miraculous meeting with the new owner of The North Face…In our culture, the emphasis is on the physical, but I put equal attention on these more subtle happenings.

So, this is an invitation to look at your life through a different lens. What makes your heart sing? What strange coincidences have occurred to you? How do you feel when you follow your intuition, and when you don't?

You do not have to believe in destiny, but you might want to try putting a little more attention when something unexpected happens. Maybe it's not 'Just a Coincidence!', but a signpost to an opportunity.

Journey's End

Trading is not Rocket Science.

I started from nothing and have had a whale of a time!

Common sense, mentorships, networking, and luck have all played their part.

I do not expect to know or be interested in everything. But conversely, do not sail ahead blindly. Be aware of what you do not know and ask for advice from people who do.

And if it has never been done before, as is so often the case in technology, then find a way to discuss it with like-minded pioneers.

Attend a conference or Seedcamp event – but discuss your idea with others you trust, hear what they have to say and then make up your own mind, listening to feedback from your heart and mind.

It has been a challenging time for businesses recently many of whom have had to re-invent themselves.

But for the entrepreneur, there have never been so many opportunities in online, local enterprise, Artificial Intelligence, and Virtual Reality.

I predict offices will be converted into multi-dwelling units for work, rest and play, with corresponding opportunities for local cafes, restaurants and leisure centres.

There will also be a desperate need for an environmentally friendly alternative to plastic, which has made a remarkable comeback due to the proliferation of protective gloves and visors.

If I was starting again today, these are the areas, given my interests, I would investigate.

But I'll leave it to you and I'm excited to see how your paths develop as Authentic Entrepreneurs!

About Stephen Kirk

Stephen Kirk has one of the first Computer Science Degrees and has seen the emergence of computer technology from its inception.

Beginning his working career as a Systems Analyst and Computer Programmer, he soon realised he was not cut out for a 'normal' career and chucked it all in to become a meditation teacher only to be struck with a sudden urge to go into business.

At the end of the meditation course, he somehow landed a prestigious European sales role, before branching out and forming Cable London plc which successfully bid for the franchises for five London Boroughs and pioneered interactive capability.

Simultaneously, he founded Broadsystem, which specialised in interactive services for media companies.

Following the sale of Broadsystem to News Corporation, Stephen worked for News for ten years before being diagnosed with and cured of colon cancer in 2000.

Since then, he has undertaken a variety of Non-Executive roles, including being on the Boards of Shine Television and The Ink Factory.

He is a Neuro-Linguistic Programming Master Practitioner, Executive Coach, amateur Blues guitarist, and a genuinely funny guy.

He and his wife Luiza live in Central London but spend many months travelling abroad looking for Paradise. Perhaps one day they'll find it!

Praise for The Authentic Entrepreneur

"I have enjoyed the journey of Stephen's life and his interviewees. It's a stimulating read and achieves its main objective (which is what I try to tell my mentees at The Princes Trust), namely follow your dream and grasp opportunities as they appear through life. Failure is simply a learning and enhancing process as a path to happiness."

Michael Rosenberg OBE, Chairman Shefa Gems Ltd, Starcom Systems ltd, Co-Founder TVAM Ltd, Director David Paradine Productions Ltd

"I have been fortunate to know Stephen since the early days of my private equity career. His story and those of the others in his book tell the reader that you can be successful whilst simultaneously being a thoroughly decent person topped off with a sense of humour. Stephen's own varied career gives a sense of perspective and teaches us all to remain focused on the bigger picture in life."

Dan Adler, partner, Apiary Capital LLP

"Stephen's track record as a brilliant businessman is clear for all to see. But over the past 20 years, I have been equally impressed by his altruism and compassion. Few executives have the wisdom to understand that the spiritual and emotional side of business has a profound bearing on corporate success. His book is compelling, convincing and persuasive. In my view, it should be essential reading for all those who run businesses - or aspire to. Whether as a board member, executive coach or delighting audiences worldwide with his entertaining and thought-provoking keynote speeches, Stephen's balanced and harmonious world view is a positive force for good. He is an honourable man and I highly recommend him."

Paul Boross, The Pitch Doctor

"I don't think Stephen knew all the rules and laws of many sports, but in business, his genius and vision knew how to play every game. His quiet wisdom and knowledge became his partner, and he imparted that knowledge to many others as well as at boardroom tables."

Colin Turner, international sports consultant and commentator

"Stephen has been an ongoing inspiration for both myself and my approach to business. He carries a depth of understanding that has its source in his explorations of the notions of being, and springs upwards through his experience and success at the highest level of business. He manages to translate his deep understandings into applicable, practical strategies for business – which I have been lucky to have received from him personally. One of the few people I always look forward to meeting, as I know we could be discussing the pitfalls of spiritual neglect and commercial tactics in the one conversation!"

Diarmuid Moloney, CEO, Rotor Videos

The Prince's Trust

It all began in 1976, when HRH The Prince of Wales had a bold idea. Having completed his duty in the Royal Navy, His Royal Highness became dedicated to improving the lives of disadvantaged young people in the UK. He founded His Trust to deliver on that commitment.

The Prince's Trust believes that every young person should have the chance to embrace exciting opportunities. The charity helps 11 to 30 year-olds to find the skills and confidence they need to explore their potential and move into work, training or education.

Since 1983, The Prince's Trust has helped more than 89,000 young people to start their own business.

The charity's Enterprise programme, which helps 18 to 30-year-olds transform their big ideas into a business reality, is made up of key stages to help young people explore if self-employment is right for them. From training and mentoring support to funding and resources, The Trust helps young people to become the best entrepreneur they can be.

More details can be found at www.princes-trust.org.uk

.

Printed in Great Britain
by Amazon

58436089R00121